## *To Be Perfectly Honest*

"This book is fabulous ar ce because my doctor doesn't w urnal
entries can help alter the v ships,
God's grace, and our own lan to
plagiarize everything Phil has written here!"

—BRYAN DUNCAN, Grammy Award–winning musician

"Reading Phil Callaway's writing is one of life's pure pleasures. His
books are not just a pleasure to savor, like eating a perfectly ripe pear.
They are full of firm insights that give grace for the daily race, especially when the journey is hard."

—ELLEN VAUGHN, *New York Times* best-selling coauthor
of *It's All About Him* and author of *Time Peace*

"Phil Callaway may be known for his humor, but he takes on a serious topic in *To Be Perfectly Honest*: He tries not to lie for one solid
year. Thankfully, he takes us along on his 365-day journey with his
sense of humor firmly intact. You'll enjoy this book—no lie."

—MARK JOSEPH, Foxnews.com, author of *The Lion,
the Professor, and the Movies: Narnia's Journey to
the Big Screen*

"Phil is what you'd get if you tampered with the genes of Garrison
Keillor, Dave Barry, and my fourth-grade Sunday school teacher.
Don't buy a copy of this book. Buy a few dozen."

—JOEL FREEMAN, author of *God Is Not Fair*, chaplain
for the Washington Bullets

# Praise for
# Phil Callaway

"I love Phil Callaway because he manages to accomplish what few writers can—masterfully blending laughter with learning."

—LEE STROBEL, best-selling author
of *The Case for Christ*

"Very few authors make me laugh out loud. Phil Callaway makes me roar. Maybe that's why I savor his books like a cup of hot chocolate. Sipping each story slowly, rolling it around my mouth to get the full flavor. Then spitting it all over the room in reaction to the hilarious truth."

—KEN DAVIS, author and comedian

"Reading Phil Callaway is like playing in holy sand. You're having so much fun you don't realize how much has gone into your shoes and is now sticking to your life."

—CHRIS FABRY, author and host of *Chris Fabry Live!*

"God speaks through the small and ordinary in extraordinary ways. Phil has listened and heard—and thankfully decided to share it with us."

—MICHAEL CARD, author, teacher, and
singer/songwriter

"Phil Callaway is master of the funny bone and the heart tug. He pretends to be just a fellow traveler, but I'm not fooled: he knows the ground well, and I'd follow him anywhere."

—MARK BUCHANAN, author of *The Rest of God*
and *Hidden in Plain Sight*

# TO BE PERFECTLY HONEST

One Man's Year of ^ALMOST Living Truthfully Could Change Your Life. No Lie.

# PHIL CALLAWAY

**Author of *Laughing Matters***

MULTNOMAH
BOOKS

To Be Perfectly Honest
Published by Multnomah Books
12265 Oracle Boulevard, Suite 200
Colorado Springs, Colorado 80921

All Scripture quotations, unless otherwise indicated, are taken from the King James Version. Scripture quotations marked (ESV) are taken from The Holy Bible, English Standard Version, copyright © 2001 by Crossway Bibles, a division of Good News Publishers. Used by permission. All rights reserved. Scripture quotations marked (MSG) are taken from The Message by Eugene H. Peterson. Copyright © 1993, 1994, 1995, 1996, 2000, 2001, 2002. Used by permission of NavPress Publishing Group. All rights reserved. Scripture quotations marked (NIV) and quotes on pages 10 and 181 are taken from the Holy Bible, New International Version®. NIV®. Copyright © 1973, 1978, 1984 by Biblica Inc.™ Used by permission of Zondervan. All rights reserved worldwide. www. zondervan.com. Scripture quotations marked (NKJV) are taken from the New King James Version®. Copyright © 1982 by Thomas Nelson Inc. Used by permission. All rights reserved. Scripture quotations marked (NLT) are taken from the Holy Bible, New Living Translation, copyright © 1996. Used by permission of Tyndale House Publishers Inc., Wheaton, Illinois 60189. All rights reserved.

Details in some anecdotes and stories have been changed to protect the identities of the persons involved.

ISBN 978-1-59052-917-1
ISBN 978-1-60142-385-6 (electronic)

Cover design by Kristopher Orr

Published in the United States by WaterBrook Multnomah, an imprint of the Crown Publishing Group, a division of Random House Inc., New York.

MULTNOMAH and its mountain colophon are registered trademarks of Random House Inc.

Library of Congress Cataloging-in-Publication Data
Callaway, Phil, 1961–
    To be perfectly honest : one man's year of almost living truthfully could change your life—no lie / Phil Callaway.—1st ed.
        p. cm.
    Includes bibliographical references (p.      ).
    ISBN 978-1-59052-917-1—ISBN 978-1-60142-385-6 (electronic)  1. Truthfulness and falsehood—Religious aspects—Christianity.  2. Callaway, Phil, 1961–  I. Title.
    BV4647.T7C35 2011
    241'.673—dc22

                                2010051163

Printed in the United States of America
2011

10  9  8  7  6  5  4  3  2

SPECIAL SALES
Most WaterBrook Multnomah books are available at special quantity discounts when purchased in bulk by corporations, organizations, and special-interest groups. Custom imprinting or excerpting can also be done to fit special needs. For information, please e-mail SpecialMarkets@WaterBrookMultnomah.com or call 1-800-603-7051.

■ ■ ■

*For all who lived near me during this wonderful,*
*traumatic year. Especially my forgiving friends.*

# CONTENTS

# The Truth Dare

Some phone calls change your Saturday; some your entire year. When my editor called, he couldn't have known he would accomplish both.

"I've had an idea for a while," said Ron. "It will make for a great book, and you're just the guy to write it."

I'm human. I was flattered.

"Is it about understanding women?" I asked. "About being sensitive to my wife's needs?"

"Why?"

"I'm good at those things, Ron. I am most excellent."

"Are you telling the truth?"

"Uh…why do you ask?"

"Well, that's what this book is about: complete and total honesty. I want you to see if you can tell the whole truth and nothing but the truth for an entire year."

"I'm sorry," I said, "you're breaking up on this end." (I pretended to hang up, and judging from the prolonged silence, he thought I had.) The truth is, as my Native American friend Roy likes to say, I had reservations.

For some, a lieless year would be an easy assignment. Their

natural habitat is the truth. Not me. I lie for a living. Oh, I'm not a used-car salesman or a politician. Nor do I write copy for bank advertisements. It's worse. I am a humorist. I stand in front of audiences and tell stories. These stories are 99¾ percent true—at least as far as I can remember. But sometimes I add just enough salt to keep a tale savory, just enough falsehood to keep people interested. Some of the things I describe may not technically have happened, but they might just as well have.

After pretending to get back on the line, I leaked all this information to Ron as if he were my priest. He seemed to listen attentively, though he could have been working a crossword puzzle, texting his wife, or reading e-mail. I told him the assignment would be complicated by the fact that I have been a chronic fudger all my life. Most people don't know this because I have become so adept at it. I fudge that I'm fudging.

And to be honest with you, I learned it at church. The church my family was part of seemed to reward falsehood. Nothing seemed to be more important than a person's outward appearance, so from an early age, I learned to fake my faith. Whenever anyone asked, I'd claim that I'd been having my devotions. I'd sing "I love to tell the story…of Jesus and His love" when I would sooner have had my eyebrows plucked by spider monkeys than talk to anyone about God.

Our church embraced an impossible system of rules, which was rigged to render you miserable, no matter what you did. Ignore the rules and you were guilt-ridden. Follow them to the letter and you ended up either self-righteous or sporting a nervous twitch. As a result, I bathed my answers to adult questions in what they preferred to hear.

"What have you been up to, Philip?" The truthful answer was, "When I haven't been coveting or gossiping, I've been lusting. And, honestly, I kind of enjoy all three." But instead I'd say, "Just struggling to memorize the gospel of John, brother."

Ron quite enjoyed hearing my confession, and instead of being discouraged by it all, he was more convinced than ever that I was the perfect author for the project. I mentioned once again that history did not weigh in on the side of my success. "My ancestors were horse traders, Ron. They sold slow animals, then got out of town fast."

"You're our guy!" he said, and we hung up.

■■■

I still wasn't sold on the idea, but I couldn't stop thinking that I would love to read such a book.

If someone else wrote it.

Following someone's yearlong experiment in telling the truth wouldn't just entertain me, it may change my thinking and—if the author were honest, vulnerable, and wise—inspire me with hope. I mentioned the book idea to friends who have known me for years. I said, "I am considering taking a truth vow." Without exception, their eyebrows shot up to their bangs, though one said, "Isn't that a bit like giving up arson for Lent?"

Yeah, sort of. But that didn't stop me from accepting the challenge. And in no time I encountered the first major drawback. Having shared openly that I was now solely a truth-telling individual, I found that some of my friends insisted on getting a straight answer to things they'd wondered about since fourth grade.

"So," one asked, "do you remember in 1983 when we rented *Rocky III* and I bought taco chips and root beer and you said you'd pay me back later?"

"I'm not sure. Is that the one with 'Eye of the Tiger'?"

"Did you pay me back?"

"Probably not," I said, handing him five bucks. I hadn't written a word, and already I was out of pocket. How much would all this honesty cost me?

Other questions troubled me even more, like could I stay happily married while being completely honest with my wife? Would people pelt me with ethical dilemmas? What are the side effects to subjecting myself to sodium Pentothal injections for a year? How honest should I be about my struggles with faith, family, and the challenges of life?

In the end I agreed to write this book for the same reason some people watch NASCAR on television. I was eager to see what would become of me. Would my life change? Would I crash?

"You sure I can't write about my expertise in understanding women?" I begged Ron during our next phone call.

"Nope," he replied. "Come on, Callaway, you can do this. Tell the truth and shame the devil. Besides, I want to read it."

And with those words, the most intriguing year of my life began.

## Author's Note

This book is a work of fact. I have, however, taken two liberties. First, I engaged in minor chronological adjustments. Second, a handful of names and minor details were changed so that I may continue to live in peace and go out in public without incident in the small community I call home. I suppose a nomadic lifestyle would be ideal for an author. You could breeze into town, point out people's inconsistencies and hypocrisies, then hightail it out of there before they discover how inconsistent and hypocritical you are. The first draft of *To Be Perfectly Honest* contained all the actual names and places, and it was really quite fun. But I realized it's like a Wal-Mart greeter pointing people to Target. Not all that smart.

# ONE

# Starting Blocks

A lie is an abomination unto the Lord,
and a very present help in trouble.

—ADLAI STEVENSON

**D**ay 1. Things are going excellently well. Have yet to tell a half truth, skirt the perimeter of a lie, or fudge at all. Haven't lusted, coveted, stolen, or even entertained an angry thought. The dog is licking my face, though. It's time to open both eyes and get out of bed.

**Day 2.** Summertime. Breakfast-on-the-front-deck time. My wife, Ramona, lavished her love on me by preparing a peanut butter on rye and waiting until I finished munching before kindly entreating me to cut the grass.

"No problem," I said, then realized I'd uttered my first lie. So I amended my previous statement.

"I'm sorry. It is a problem, but I'll do it."

She grinned and rolled her eyes. "This is gonna be a long year, isn't it?"

Cutting grass does not offer a chance to lie about anything, but you can break several other commandments while chasing a lawn mower. The one about coveting, for instance. My neighbor Neil keeps his grass tourist green, like a refurbished Disney cartoon. He frames his yard with a perfectly rounded hedge, and the diagonal lines in his lawn are ruler straight, like Wrigley Field. How does he do this? With GPS?

Mowing my lawn is also a recipe for anger, and not just anger at myself for not moving the stupid garden hose before I ran over it. For some reason repetitive behavior brings out the worst in me. While my mind is on autopilot, it rarely steers me toward the "whatever things" of Scripture.[1] Instead, I think of people who wronged me back in elementary school or a nasty note that arrived last week. I think of seeking vengeance on my enemies, of pouring weedkiller on their lawns or damaging their reputations with anonymous leaflets dropped from light aircraft.

Some people have imaginary friends. When I cut the grass, I have imaginary enemies. I fabricate conversations in which I deliver brilliant responses to their accusations. More than any place else, it is my own backyard where I have to wonder: am I even a Christian?

What I need is a diversion, and sure enough…

Two men are coming up the walk, sporting suits and ties. It's Saturday, for Pete's sake. I power down my Briggs and Stratton. The visitors have nametags and introduce themselves and offer me their scriptures. Try as I might, I can't resist the thing that is welling up inside me. I know I shouldn't, but I do. I stretch out my hands—not to take the book they are offering, but to do some fake sign language. I point to my ears and shake my head and mouth the word "deaf."

"I guess he's deaf," says the smarter one. They smile, frown, then walk away.

I think they know I can hear. (The headphones from my iPod might have tipped them off.)

I'll bet they're talking about what a complete pagan I am. A guy who is such a hard-core liar that he doesn't even need words. A guy who is so beyond hope that even if I applied for membership and confessed and had references, they would deny me entry into their church.

How will I ever make it even one day without lying? I've already lied and it's only Saturday. At least everything I've written so far is true.

Everything except the part about the Mormons. While it's true that I was mowing my lawn on a Saturday and thinking terrible things, I imagined the part about acting deaf and dumb, which I'm sure would really be fun. What a tragedy to have such a great story roadblocked by the truth.

Is it too late to start over on this book project? Why not? Tomorrow can be day one.

**Day 1b.** Nothing much to report. A really good day. I had a horrible canker on the inside of my lip, and it hurt like a shark bite when I talked. Perhaps that helped. No lies today. Church was quite good, the worship music a nice blend of old and new. The sermon was brief but meaty.

Afterward, Henry asked me to head up the adult Sunday school department, and I said, "No. I can't." That's all. I didn't concoct an elaborate excuse involving illness, death, or a son's imaginary tuba recital.

I'm really optimistic. I think this project is doable.

**Day 2b.** An acquaintance from the Deep South sent me an e-mail. I asked if he had any good possum recipes. He asked if it's cold where I live. "It's warm now," I told him, "but in the winter, the men huddle around in a tight circle, holding our children on our feet." He didn't get it. I guess he's never seen *March of the Penguins*.

Is it a lie if you're obviously joking? This could be a long year if it is.

**Day 3.** Living truthfully delivers clear benefits, like not having to keep my lies straight. I told my buddy Regi about my truth project, and he asked if it was okay to tell others about it. He meant people who have known me through the years, people who may want to contact me with questions. I told him sure, it was no problem.

"Are you really going to do this?" he asked.

"Of course I am."

"Will you tell the absolute truth about anything I ask you?"

"Of course I will."

Regi said we should get together for coffee. Should be fun, though there are things I'd rather not talk about. What if he asks about the time—? Naw. He wouldn't dare. But I wonder: when a friend asks you about past events, can you just say, "Pass," like you're a baseball player testifying before Congress?

**Days 4, 5.** Very little to report. Told nothing but the truth and barely flinched.

**Day 6.** Saw a Jerry Seinfeld quote: "I think that people who read the tabloids deserve to be lied to."

**Day 7.** My mother-in-law asked if I'd like to come over for supper. Questions like this one can be problematic. Rather than answer immediately, should I ask her to rephrase her question? And what will I say if Ramona asks, "Sweetheart, do the horizontal stripes on this outfit make me look husky?"

And it's not just family either. I have friends who are starting to ask hard questions. Do I tell a friend who struggles with his weight that when he walks past, it looks like two leopards are wrestling in his pants? Certainly not. All truth is not to be told at all times. And frankly, who has time to answer everyone's questions with a lot of detail? So maybe I should change the message on my answering machine: "I've reached that time of life when I've decided to make some changes. If you don't hear back from me, I guess you're one of the changes."

I'll give it some thought.

**Day 8.** Great sermon today, but suddenly my mind did a right turn, and I was thinking about all the fun I like to have on the phone. Will my truth vow prohibit me from playing jokes while using a Chinese accent?

**Day 9.** Got a Facebook friend request today from an East Coast romance novelist I met two years ago at a writers' conference. At the time, she confessed that she'd had a dream about me. As she described it, with her hypnotic blue eyes dancing, the dream sounded straight out of one of her novels.

It took a full month to purge her dream from my head. What was I doing listening to it? I accepted her Facebook friend request, though. One never knows. It could present a good witnessing opportunity.

**Day 10.** If I am to tell the unpolished truth and live with complete integrity all year, must I pay back those I have wronged or cheated in the past? Does this mean apologizing to fellow golfers who thought I beat them fair and square, when in truth I cheated? How many years back does one go? Isn't there a statute of limitations on this sort of thing? My entire year could be spent confessing past sins.

At the very least, I'll make things right as God brings them to mind. I decided to pray about it, and God immediately brought to mind my friend Arlen. Twenty years ago I didn't pay him back for a lunch, so I called and agreed to dinner and golf.

I'll kill two birds with one checkbook.

**Day 11.** I sent an e-mail notice to some friends telling them about the book project. "I cannot tell a lie for 365 days," I wrote. "Ask me anything. Hook up the wires and tweak the dials."

Big mistake. Seems some of them forwarded my note to others, and questions have been arriving all day.

My brother Tim wrote: "Since you're sworn to honesty all year, do you or do you not owe me money?"

I told him the truth: "No." And reminded him of the hundred dollars he still owes me from when we were kids and he was forever offering me quarters to bug off.

Ellen asked, "Do you honestly think you can be that honest that long?"

I admitted: "I have my doubts but am opting for optimism."

Jane (whom my wife baby-sat many years ago) wondered if I still listen to ABBA. "You got me hooked as a child!" she charged.

I wrote her back: "Mamma mia! Does your mother know about your problem? I thought you were writing to say, 'Thank you for the music, the songs I'm singin'. Thanks for all the joy they're bringin'.' But no. Do I take the blame? I do, I do, I do, I do, I do. Knowing me, knowing you, it's the best I can do. Soon I hope you'll be as good as new."[2]

**Day 12.** Our three college kids have flown home to our empty nest for a rare weekend together. We miss our children when they're away, though the dog doesn't miss them jumping out of closets and scaring the cookies out of her.

They're all single, and our daughter, Rachael, has pasted a Bible verse on her door: "Be merciful to me, O God, for men hotly pursue me" (Psalm 56:1).

A little out of context, methinks.

**Day 14.** Had devotions this morning. Honest.

**Day 15.** I was asked to pray in church today. Quite an honor. I thanked God for our church; the people in it; the music; the fellowship; the health to be here, far from hunger and persecution. And then I realized I wasn't praying to God at all. I was praying to the people, hoping to impress them. "Wow, that Callaway sure is a good pray-er, we should have him pray more often! Every Sunday, perhaps."

My truth vow is starting to give me Pharisee's Itch.[3]

"Amen," I said, a little too abruptly. And sat down.

**Day 16.** I wonder if missionaries from the church based in Salt Lake City, who ride mountain bikes and wear backpacks and travel in pairs, ever come to our sleepy community. I wonder what I'd say to one if I ever had the chance.

**Day 17.** My friend Regi and I went out for coffee. "Isn't grace a wonderful thing?" I observed. "Aren't you thankful that our sins are forgiven, that nothing we've done can be held against us? Grace is something we need to give thanks for and practice too, don't you think?"

Regi grinned widely and said, "So you're gonna tell the truth, eh?"

Regi is Canadian.

"Yup."

"Do you remember when I asked you how you recorded such crystal-clear copies of the Sherlock Holmes TV shows they ran on PBS?"

"I think so. Yes, I do."

"You said the reception was real good that week. Did you copy them illegally?"

I coughed nervously. "Yes, I did."

"I thought so."

"I'm sorry. I will get rid of them."

The rest of our time went well. Still, I wonder if some other time he might bring up the other things I've been worried about. One can only hope he's forgotten.

**Day 18.** I decided to read up on the doctrines of the missionaries who didn't visit while I was mowing the lawn. I looked up their church on the Internet, watched some YouTube debates, and couldn't resist sending an e-mail just for fun:

A week ago I had a visit from two of your young men while I was cutting the grass. They were dressed very sharply and were very kind to me. Regrettably, I was not kind to them. In fact, I pretended that I was deaf (maybe you've heard

about it). I would love to find some way to apologize to them.
Are you able to suggest a way I can contact them? Feel free
to send them by. I'll be kinder to them this time. Thanks so
much. I live in…

Will I have to stop this kind of joking? Probably.

**Day 19.** I picked up a copy of *Time* magazine during the time I
usually reserve for devotions. It said, "There is no other single force
causing as much measurable hardship and human misery in this
country as the collapse of marriage."[4] God doesn't speak to me often
through news magazines, but I almost heard an audible voice telling
me to ask Ramona out to dinner.

She said there was already something cooking.

"Throw it out, cool it down, or freeze it, baby," I said in my best
Harrison Ford/Indiana Jones imitation. "My engine's revvin'."

She snickered. Her cheeks flushed. The whole evening went very
well.

I wore a fedora; that helped.

Twenty-seven years we've been married. It has been an adven-
ture, to say the least. Ramona deals with sporadic seizures that
throw her out of commission for a week each time they take hold.
Thankfully, they've been rare as possum recipes lately, but they
keep us on our knees, aware that we don't control much that really
matters.

**Day 21.** Cut the grass and no Mormons showed up. I have
something I'd like to try on them. It would make for a great story.

Today I received an invitation to speak at a public-school teach-
ers' convention coming up in the spring. They must not know I'm a
Christian. Have I been hiding it under a bushel that thoroughly?
Should I tell them before or after I arrive? What will I say when I
speak? "Our educational system is broken, and today I'd like to talk

about bringing back three items: moral absolutes, prayer, and Scripture memorization"? Will the sound man slowly turn down the PA system, or will they all rise up in unison and pelt me with atheist textbooks?

What shall I title my talk? "Daniel in the Teachers' Den"?

I once spent a week preparing to speak at a couples' retreat—some pretty good stuff on marriage and child-rearing—only to arrive and discover the conferees were single.

Note to self:

a) Know your audience.

b) Update life insurance policy and will.

**Day 22.** Church had just let out when a woman came up to me in the foyer. She told me she thought I was pretty hot and that she wanted to be the mother of my children.

I said, "Whoa, honey! Cool it! I'm almost fifty; you'll give me an angina attack."

All these years I've been married to her and still these surprises.

**Day 23.** Was going to read a C. S. Lewis book to expand my mind and strengthen my faith. But decided to play Pac-Man instead. I was doing quite well at it, navigating the maze, gulping dots, tossing back little blue creatures, confident about reaching my highest score ever, perhaps scaling the seventeenth level.

Then the stupid power went off, and there wasn't a storm in sight. We've paid our utility power bill. Surely God wouldn't plunge the whole town into darkness just to teach me a time-management lesson, would he?

I groped my way into our dark bedroom and sat down on a hardback book. As I picked it up, the lights flickered and power was restored. I was holding a copy of *Mere Christianity*. I briefly considered hurrying back to my study and trying to reach level thirteen, but wondered if God might employ lightning this time.

## Honest Confession #1

Already I've been reminded that I am proud, mischievous, and evasive. I came to faith in Christ precisely because I am a broken person who does not naturally lead a disciplined, honest, and humble life. And if you think things are bad now, it hasn't even been a full month yet.

# TWO

# The Lost Art of Confrontation

No man has a good enough memory to make
a successful liar.

—ABRAHAM LINCOLN

**D**ay 24. I caught a few minutes of the TV show *Intervention*. An addict was made to believe he was being filmed for a documentary, then family and friends jumped out of closets for a dramatic confrontation. It was heartbreaking, really. And ironically, addictive. The show follows an extra-biblical mandate: "If a brother sins against you, broadcast it for millions to watch."

I've always received poor marks in Confronting Class. I was the youngest of five, so peacekeeping kept me alive. I learned early not to face my eldest brother, David, with the fact that smoking cigarettes turned his breath to compost and hurt his dating chances. This turned out badly the first time I tried it. He pummeled my tiny body with fists the size of mallets.

Even now, having watched a number of friends sabotage their lives, I would rather knit a football field–sized comforter than say,

"You know, I think you spend too much time golfing. Your wife hasn't seen you since 2004." I should have done this with one friend. A year later, when he left his wife and sons, I kicked myself for a month. If I am to live the lieless life, I must show drastic improvement in my confrontational skills.

Back in the 1980s during a South African parliamentary debate, P. W. Botha, the prime minister who was called the Great Crocodile, growled, "The honorable member from Houghton, it is well known, does not like me." The honorable member, Helen Suzman, stood to her full height of five feet two, and said, "Like you? I cannot stand you."

I wonder what will happen if I employ this kind of blunt honesty.

**Day 25.** I had devotions again and read, "If thy brother trespass against thee, rebuke him."[1]

This was no coincidence. It's time to take the honesty thing to a new level. Where would I be if people hadn't faced me with my shortcomings?

I decided to try being brutally honest with at least one person today. I would speak with love, of course, but love would not keep me from speaking the truth. Jesus did this. But maybe that was easy for him because he didn't have a wife.

Nevertheless, I shouldn't shy away from rebuking—and the nearest person around is my wife. Although strictly speaking, she is a sister, not a brother, I decided I'd rebuke her about her…um… I'm not sure. About the meal last night? It was quite good. Her attitude? She's been humming while sweeping the floor. We've been getting along quite famously of late. Perhaps I'll just take things as they come and not plan these assignments.

**Day 26.** I went to visit my mother and, as always, was reminded that dementia isn't much fun for anyone. She mostly remembers who

I am when I visit, but forgets basic stuff like my name, where she lives, and whether or not at eighty-five, she's pregnant.

"I'm expecting," she told me today, then frowned at my apparent lack of faith. "Abraham and Sarah did it," she insisted.

Mom taught me about the birds and the bees and other assorted insects when I was in fourth grade, but she endeavored to tell me again today. This is not something I woke up this morning hoping to hear, particularly now that she seems to have things a little mixed up.

I've found it's best to go along with her stories, to ask how she's feeling now that she's pregnant, whether she battles morning sickness, and what she will name the child.

"Is it a boy or girl?" I asked.

"It's twins!" she said. "One of both!"

My wife liked chocolate when she was pregnant, so I found some for Mom. As she munched it, I rambled on about my day and the kids and my wife and my work—the same things I had told her a few days ago. The beauty of dementia is that everything is fresh—reading faded old magazines from 1999 has you asking your son to buy you Y2K supplies and getting rather excited about the end of the world.

**Day 27.** More e-mails arrived from friends who seemed concerned about me telling them the truth.

Verna, a friend of my mother's, asked: "I can never tell when you're (a) telling the truth, (b) lying, or (c) being facetious. Are you really writing a book of diary entries?"

Joel wrote, "What is your worst nightmare?" The truth is, I have had three recurring nightmares in my life:

1. Being chased by Communists and being unable to run
2. Not being able to find my ice hockey skates during an important game against the Communists

3. Most recently, standing in front of a large audience, possibly
   Communists, stark raving naked and without notes and
   not a word coming out of my mouth making any sense

Jodie asked: "Do you ever make up statistics?" Answer: "No,
but I've heard that 74 percent of statistics are made up on the spot."

**Day 28.** The afternoon was spent shopping with my wife and
daughter. "You have too many shoes already," I said, which was met
with icy stares from both. Maybe I'm better at confronting than I
thought.

"Rachael, you're boy crazy."

"Am not." She grinned. "But my favorite TV show is *Mantracker*."

I looked around the store for others to confront. Most seemed
hurried and a little scared. The employees behind the tills all seemed
to need encouragement more than anything. I found myself being
nice to them.

My daughter asked if I was okay. Of course I am.

**Day 29.** I sat in the front row of the church where I was speaking. The gal leading worship was wearing a dress that was hiked up
to the Mississippi River Delta. Is it possible I was the only one who
noticed this? Perhaps. If I mentioned it to anyone, would I be told I
have problems? Probably. Should I have confronted her husband
rather than her? Most certainly. Was I glad I was the visiting speaker
and got to flee town two hours later? You bet.

**Day 30.** Major-league blow today: I was told that economic
woes have devalued my retirement savings plan by 50 percent. It's
like someone showed up with a giant chain saw and split my house
in two, then shoved half of it off a cliff.

I pulled out the calculator and found I can now retire at the age
of 132.

My neighbor asked how I'm doing. Horrendous. Dreadful.
Horrific.

"Fine," I said. "How are you?" Will I ever stop with the knee-jerk lying?

And as if things aren't bad enough, it looks like I'll have to trust God for my finances. Shoot! It has come to this.

**Day 31.** I received more e-mail input from friends who are taking advantage of this opportunity to hook me up to the self-inflicted lie detector. Actually, I thought their questions would be harder. If I could ask me anything on earth, I'd ask about deeper, darker stuff.

Neil wanted to hear about my most embarrassing moment, and Nick wondered about my biggest fear. Aaron wrote, "Many years ago, I was fishing with my dad on Pine Lake when some smart aleck in a passing boat called out, 'Hey, you guys using hooks?' It was you. So, a question to test the truth-telling: what is the largest fish you ever caught?"

Steve, one of my best childhood buddies, asked, "Phil, do you ever fear your childhood friends will try to blackmail you with all the misdeeds we know you've committed?"

Here are my honest answers,

Neil: I once deliberately frightened a man whom I thought was someone else. I awoke with a snort during a sermon (not one of mine). I really do wish my embarrassing moments were juicier.

Nick: My biggest fear, apart from wolves, is of peanut butter sticking to the roof of my mouth. Okay, that's not it. My biggest fear is that I might end up not practicing what I preach.

Aaron: I have no recollection of questioning your nonuse of hooks while fishing. My biggest catch was a five-pound rainbow trout. Caught it with a hook.

Steve: Yes, absolutely. I sometimes think of Chuck Rogers, a childhood friend who is now a successful lawyer. I once stole money from him. I hope he's as forgiving as you are.

**Day 32.** Ramona mentioned that she had booked me for a "little procedure" at the medical clinic at 10 a.m. tomorrow. It will ensure that surprises are kept to a minimum and we don't have to buy Pampers with our pension checks. I'll get to spend a few days recovering afterward, she said, maybe reading the entire Old Testament twice, then watching five seasons of *Lost*.

In this case, I have no trouble being brutally honest with her.

A friend called just after dinner to tell me that three guys need a fourth for golf tomorrow. The weather should be gorgeous. Tee time is 10 a.m., and my friend will buy lunch. Of course, I felt at complete and total peace about it. I quickly took the phone to the other room and answered, "YES! COUNT ME IN!"

"Who was that?" asked Ramona.

"Oh, just Mike. He...uh...wants to get together."

If I tell a tiny portion of the truth, is it still a lie?

**Day 33.** I have golfed with celebrities, with authors, with stars. I have won tournaments in two countries and come within a quarter inch of a $10,000 hole-in-one. But I have never savored a game of golf more than I did today.

Ramona just shook her head when I asked if we could reschedule my medical appointment. "What do you mean, we?" she said. "Do you have worms?"

"Hey, you learned that line from me."

I wondered if I should confront her about her attitude.

**Day 34.** I did it to myself. I asked people to send in any question they wanted me to answer, with the promise that I would respond truthfully. It's like releasing rabbits into a cheetah cage.

A letter arrived today from Terence Doerksen, a guy I knew throughout high school. Terence and his wife serve Jesus in central Asia, and he enclosed a picture of him and his family riding an elephant and trying to feign terror. I will quote the second paragraph of the accompanying letter.

Do you remember the time in ninth grade when we rode our ten speeds east of town, then stripped down and ran around on the rocks dressed just like we were when we came into this world?

This whole thing is getting out of hand. Should I change my address?

**Day 36.** Can't remember what the sermon was about today. Maybe trust or worry or the limitations of money. I was too busy panicking over thoughts of our sinking investments and my stolen retirement. "Why me, Lord? Help! Please!"

**Day 38.** Midmorning I called my friend Robert, the only Mormon I know, and asked if we could go out for lunch. "Can't today," he said.

The church headquarters must have forwarded my lighthearted e-mail to him as a warning. I think he knows.

**Day 41.** Opportunities to confront people are popping up everywhere. Today Dan Adkins—a golfing buddy whom I have suspected of cheating for years—called. He was tempting me to play a round.

"No way," I said. "You cheat." I was trying to be serious.

He laughed. No one takes a humorist seriously.

I suddenly realized: His call is no coincidence. This is a God-given opportunity.

We golfed nine holes in two hours. I watched him like a hawk. Twice he found a hopelessly lost ball in the rough. I was positive he was dropping a replacement ball to the ground, making use of a convenient hole in his shorts.

I confronted him. No sir, the guy was as clean as fresh sheets. I couldn't believe I was disappointed to find that he's so honest.

On the eighth hole, he pointed across the creek and said, "Look at that coyote!" I blinked several times but couldn't see it. Dan's eyes are laser sharp. No wonder he can find the ball. I hit my ball thirty yards and I need a guide dog.

**Day 42.** My eldest son brought a friend home for dinner. He was unusually helpful in the kitchen, loading the dishwasher, sweeping the floor, asking, "Is there anything I can do?"

"You must be interested in my daughter," I joked.

He grinned and laughed a little too loudly.

**Day 43.** Call me cranky, but I decided not to join in on a few of the worship songs in church this morning. I feel too much like a liar when I do. We were singing, "You're all I want, you're all I've ever needed…,"[2] and I couldn't help thinking of all the things I want. I want my children to be okay, I want health, I want enough money for lunch at the sub shop, I want a nicer car, I want to take a winter vacation.

Then the leader strummed the opening chords for "Better is one day in your house…than thousands elsewhere…,"[3] and I knew I couldn't, in good conscience, sing that one either. I could think of a dozen places I'd rather be than in church.

"Shout to the Lord…"[4] I hadn't heard a shout in this church since the children took the stage for the Christmas program and Danny E. had toilet paper hanging out the back of his pants.

"We lift our hands…"[5] Sorry. Not in our church. I am part of a denomination where we lift our hands only during a police raid, though we haven't had the opportunity to test my theory.

I've been longing for the good old songs I can understand, like "Here I raise my Ebenezer…"[6]

The singing continued, and I found myself mouthing some words—just in case others noticed that I hadn't been singing and considered me less spiritual.

**Day 44.** While still pouting at the bad news on the financial front and the prospects of being a ninety-nine-year-old Wal-Mart greeter, a letter arrived from our sponsored child in Rwanda. He is fifteen and in sixth grade. He asked us to pray that his mother will find enough food today. He wanted to buy some crutches for his sister. He wanted us to send a picture of where we live.

Suddenly I had a revised financial-themed prayer:

> Thank you, Lord, that I have lost half of my retirement
> savings. You already know it, but I've been turning my eyes
> from the Blesser to the blessings, from the Giver to the gifts.
> I've liked stuff. I've thought it was the best defense against
> aging, against chance. I've confused my wants with my
> needs. I've chased what I don't have, forgetting what you gave
> me. Remind me that this life is a short and fevered practice
> for a game I can't stay to play. Keep me ever mindful of the
> eternal, ever aware of the needs of others. I'll buy those
> crutches. I promise. Amen.

**Day 45.** I crafted a response to my high school friend Terence Doerksen, my ten-speed-riding streaker buddy who now resides in Asia.

> I am sorry but the middle part of your letter had severe
> water damage and was therefore illegible. I did enjoy the
> rest of it, however. Glad to know you're doing well and
> in good health. What great memories I have of our high
> school years together. Do you remember the time we went
> door to door, telling others of our faith? I can't remember
> if we rode bicycles or how we were dressed. Modestly, I am
> quite certain. Modesty was big for us back then, wasn't it?
> I remember some of our classmates struggled in this area,
> but not us. No sir.

Is this a lie? I don't think so. A few weeks and I'll hear him laughing all the way from central Asia.

**Day 46.** My class reunion is coming up next week. Can't believe it's been thirty years since I hoisted my high school diploma, then spent the summer trying to grow a mustache. A guy I haven't seen in a quarter century e-mailed me this nugget he found in the classifieds:

> Love-starved SWM seeking trophy wife with upper-
> class looks and attitude to take to my next high school
> reunion.

I'm thankful for a wife who is a complete babe. If just one of my classmates leers at her or asks if she's my daughter, I swear I'll start a fight with my cane.

**Day 47.** E-mails keep arriving from folks who say they're thrilled with the opportunity to hear a humorist come clean.

MacKenzie asked about the most embarrassing thing I did in front of my wife while I was courting her. I imagine MacKenzie was hoping for a juicier tidbit, but all I can think of is our first kiss.

"It was a disaster. I missed most of her mouth because I was thinking of how badly I would feel when she rejected me because of my bad technique (which I had practiced on my hand, and once on a balloon)."

Brenda asked, "So…have you ever pretended to like something Ramona had cooked for you but really didn't and lied so as not to hurt her feelings? Oh, and have you ever had curlers in your hair or a perm? It was very popular even for guys in the 1970s."

My honest response: "Brenda, my wife is an exceptional cook. Really. Of course, even Mozart threw out some sheet music. So yes, I have had to pretend to enjoy a few items of her cooking, and we've had at least one fight over soup. Split pea, I believe. The color was suspect. I have never had a perm or tried curlers. Once my daughter tried dying my hair, but it stayed gray. It's that dead."

Ellen wondered what I think will be the first piece of advice I'll offer my first grandchild.

"Ellen, I'd like them to learn by experience, so I think I shall say, 'Hey, why don't you bring that cat over here? I'll show you how to play the bagpipes. Put the tail in your mouth, like this…"

**Day 48.** Is there ever a time in marriage for fudging the truth? Probably not, but Ramona told a sweet little lie today. She said, "I like you better with less hair."

I told her a little lie in return: "I like your haircut."

**Day 50.** Yes! Finally an opportunity to confront someone! And at church!

Actually, a friend calls it "carefrontation." I confront you, but I do this in a caring and compassionate way. It's like *Intervention*, but without cameras.

Confrontation, this wise friend maintains, advocates the use of shame, often leaving both participants feeling like vitamins are stuck in their throats. Carefrontation, on the other hand, is presented in the spirit of love and concern, addressing the behavior more than the behavioree.

After the morning service, Jerry Root walked up to me in the foyer, steamed that our church is spending money on a new carpet and kitchen renovations. "We should spend more money on the poor in this community," he said, shaking his head.

I took a deep breath. My pulse was racing. I asked Jerry what percentage of his income goes to the poor. It was a little abrupt, perhaps, but got the point across.

Suddenly Jerry had to talk with someone else.

I felt like there was a vitamin C tablet wedged in my throat.

Who said this would be easy? Truth-tellers, even ones who carefully use carefrontation, rarely win popularity contests.

If I were asked to pray in church today, would I be honest enough to pray this: "Forgive me, Lord. This week I have thought more about money than I have thought about you"?

**Day 51.** Class reunion is just days away. It's ridiculous trying to impress people after all these years. If they can't accept me for the guy I've become, it's their loss. I am no longer the shallow, self-absorbed, insecure kid they knew all those years ago.

Still, I spent a little more time than usual in front of the mirror, trying to figure out my best angles. If I tilt my head slightly to the left, depending on the light, my nose almost looks straight and the mole by my right eye is hardly noticeable.

Flexing is laughable; nothing happens anymore when I flex. But puffing out my chest just a touch subtracts a few years, adds a sense of good health, and hints at a lifetime of fine posture.

It's a good thing my daughter left some of these dental white strips in the bathroom, though, as I think I'm starting to see a difference when I grit my teeth.

**Day 52.** Today I will be so honest that I will say everything that comes to mind immediately and let the chips fall where they may.

7:32 a.m. The alarm went off. "Good morning," said Ramona, a little too cheerily.

"What's good about it?"

She hadn't opened her eyes yet. "Well, we're alive. We have food." It's not a bad point.

"I don't wanna get up."

"Suit yourself."

"I want breakfast. In bed."

"Ha." She rolled over and was sound asleep within moments.

7:34 a.m. I abandoned my Mind Leak project to avoid being fired in an hour and possibly having to live on the street.

**Day 53.** With only two days to go before the class reunion, I have contracted a late-onset pimple. Today I spent a few minutes questioning God's goodness.

The Lord brought to mind Chuck Rogers, my childhood friend turned lawyer. Must make that right with him about the money I stole.

With just a few e-mails to friends, I obtained Chuck's address and wrote him a note jammed with lots of good humor. I apologized for my childhood theft and offered to make it right.

What if he figures it out? Five dollars compounded over all these years could sink me, given my recent financial lack of success.

**Day 54.** With the reunion tomorrow, I'm wishing I had started an orphanage after high school. Or donated $1 million to a third world nation. Or had a picture to show them of me with Bono.

I decided to shave the tangled forest that was my eyebrows. Not sure I'm happy with the outcome. It makes me look like I got too close to a barbecue grill. Can't cover the fact that I've put on a good twenty pounds through the years, but I will go with vertical stripes on my shirt.

Stupid dental strips. I've been using triple the recommended dosage for a week now and should have read the warning label. Seems the concentration of peroxide and the duration of exposure have combined to cause extreme tooth sensitivity.

Hope they don't serve anything cold at the reunion. Or hot. Ice cream feels like a dental drill.

I told the homeschooled kid next door about the class reunion. "Wow," he said. "Thirty years is twice my age!"

I asked him how many he thinks will attend his reunion. He contemplated my words but didn't get the joke.

## Honest Confession #2

For much of my life, I spent too much time trying to impress others. But that is changing—perhaps too rapidly. My daughter says the new, more-honest me is a more-grouchy me, that I've been a little blunt the last little while. I'm glad she told me this, and I think she's right. Sometimes we need to tell ourselves the truth before we tell it to others. The truth is, being right is nice—but it's all a little pointless without good relationships. I'm sure I haven't learned the last of this.

# THREE

# How to Tell the Truth and Still Have a Place to Sleep

Never go to bed mad. Stay up and fight.

—PHYLLIS DILLER

He who tells a lie is...forced to invent twenty more to maintain that one.

—ALEXANDER POPE

**D**ay 55. Arrived for the reunion to find that some of my classmates have aged horribly. A couple of guys are almost unrecognizable and completely bald. I kept a hat on for most of the event, in case the sun came out and got in my eyes.

One of the girls told me she had a crush on me in tenth grade, that life as a writer must be fascinating, and that I'm the only real celebrity she knows. I found myself unable to stop grinning for half an hour.

Here are the top five lies told at a class reunion:

- You haven't changed a bit!
- I invented Post-it notes.
- You've lost a little weight, haven't you?
- You're far too young to have grandchildren!
- We should do this every year.

We ate s'mores and told stories around a campfire. The same guys were talking that always talked a lot. Guys like me. The guys that got good grades just listened, checking their BlackBerries to update their investment portfolios.

It's surprising what pranks one will admit to after thirty years and you're confident the statute of limitations has expired. No longer do we wonder who put the bugging apparatus in the girls' lounge (John Wall), who raised the security guard's bicycle up the flagpole (John and me), or who was responsible for the Ex-Lax epidemic of '78 (me).

Twice I found myself glancing at the girl who flattered me and wondering what life would have been like had I married her. Would we have children? What would they look like? Would they have her eyes or my nose? Would she nag me or want more stuff than I could provide? Would she have encouraged me to get a dog or take up golf like my wife had?

I mentioned my thoughts to Ramona as we climbed into bed. She smirked and asked, "What happened to your eyebrows?"

**Day 56.** Already I've slipped back into my old ways. Today I rated one of my own videos on the Internet. I gave it five stars. Excellent! *Prodigiosus!*

Felt guilty immediately, but couldn't undo the rating, except to give the same video another rating of no stars, which doesn't exactly help.

I wonder if it's possible to write a review of your own video. Sure enough: "Wow, isn't this guy funny? You should check out his Web site! Great deals on books there!"

Has it ever been easier to lie to more people? The Internet has made it possible to review your own books or set up a Web site that is all about you, then concoct your own bio and doctor the photos so you have hair.

I canceled the video review, but it felt good for a minute. Where do ideas like these come from?

Ramona has no trouble with honesty. Really. Today the gal at the restaurant accepted two twenties from my wife and gave her fifty-five dollars in change. What an answer to prayer! What a provision! I can use this as a great sermon illustration. A modern-day retelling of the Old Testament prophet Elijah and the widow whose oil and flour wouldn't run out! But no.

"I gave you two twenties, didn't I?" asks Ramona. "Just keep the change."

It's a good thing she does our taxes.

**Day 57.** In church this morning, someone thought it was a good idea for the congregation to sing "Amazing Grace" to the melody of the *Gilligan's Island* theme song. Something for the kids. I would have poked my eyes out with a sharp object, but there were no pencils in our pew. What's next? Merging this timeless classic with "Peaceful Easy Feeling"? I'm told it can be done.

We sang another song declaring that we all felt like dancing, but no one did. A number of us did sort of bend our knees a little, as if we're riding some rough waves. Next was "Lord, I Lift Your Name on High," which I'd always loved until my friend Vance told me you can sing the bass line to Steve Miller's "The Joker" perfectly with it. Complete with the "wooot-woooh."

The closing song lyrics went something like this:

"Your will. Oh Lord, we long to do your will." (Repeat nine times, then fade.)

On the way home, I thought about driving off a cliff, but we live in uncliffish country, and I'm bolstered by thoughts of the roast Ramona has simmering in the Crock-Pot.

**Day 59.** A few more questions came in from e-mail friends. This from Gabby: "Mr. Callaway, do you read your own books?"

Are you kidding, Gabby? All the time. I have been such a blessing to myself. Okay, I'll be truthful. No, I don't. Except for editing purposes and audio editions. Does that count? I once interviewed Christian author Barbara Johnson, who told me that when she was depressed, she'd find a quiet spot and read one of her books. But I prefer the Psalms.

Mary wondered: "Do you sometimes regret the loss of anonymity that comes with being an author and speaker?"

Yes, Mary. It's a horrible burden to bear. I was in a restaurant once and someone came right over and said, "Excuse me, are you—" And I said, "Yes. I'm Phil Callaway. I'd be happy to sign something for you." She looked at me a little strangely and said, "Are you done with the ketchup?"

**Day 60.** I've decided to lay aside the term *rebuke* in favor of complete honesty in my marriage. Tonight Ramona overcooked the hand-shucked peas something fierce, which is technically not a sin against me, but certainly a hardship and an opportunity to be honest.

First, though, I reminded myself that she rarely overcooks things. This is like Phil Mickelson missing a three-inch putt or Rembrandt painting something mediocre.

But on principle, I must point it out to her. Carefully. I did this once before when her mother was over and the dessert wasn't right. Things were icy around here for at least a week.

"The peas are sort of…uh…yellowish," I said. Which they were.

"They're fine," she insisted. Which they weren't.

"No, they are overcooked." I was pushing them around with a salad fork. "I'm just being honest."

Ramona was lighting candles after slaving away on a meal of honey lemon chicken, fried whole-grain rice, garden salad with three choices of dressing, and oh yes, peas that tasted like they'd been marinated in prune juice, then frozen and run through three cycles in the dishwasher.

"Honey, it's okay. Just admit it. You overcooked the peas. You had one bad pitch. You're allowed that. Just say, 'I cooked the peas a half hour too long.'"

She grew quiet, held a lit match, and wondered where to place it.

I was describing the peas in gentle, playful tones. But it was not funny to my wife.

I decided to play my ultimate trump card. "Okay, tell me this. Would you serve the peas if Jesus were visiting?"

"Yes."

"You would?"

"Jesus would eat them. And he wouldn't complain. He'd be thankful. He would focus on the chicken and rice."

I won an argument back in 1994. Not this one.

I think the groveling and sweeping floors and doing dishes helps. And saying, "I am sorry I was wrong for not eating the stupid peas, what can I do to make it up to you?"

It's easy to get mad at me, but not to stay mad at me. Still, things are a little frosty around here.

**Day 61.** Most mornings Ramona gets me breakfast, but not today.

"There are peas in the fridge," she said. "Help yourself."

At lunch I took a medium cup at a fast-food joint when I only paid for a small. Didn't mean to, of course, so I had to go back. It was a forty-nine-cent difference. The gal behind the counter seemed a little dazed when I handed her the money.

I should keep a running tally so I'll know how much a full year of honesty costs me. So far: $60.49, which includes paying back a friend, being honest in a restaurant, and now this.

Got some nice Facebook messages tonight about a story I'd written on the passing of my father. One comment came from the hypnotic East Coast romance novelist I met at a writers' conference. Said she finds me sensitive and funny.

Kinda nice of her.

The pea thing has peeved Ramona. "Sensitive" and "kind" are not words she has used in a while. I reminded her that unforgiveness is like drinking rat poison, then standing around waiting for the rat to die. Her chilly response reminded me that the $60.49 is the least of my worries.

**Day 62.** I checked Facebook and noticed another message from the East Coast: "Looks like I'll be up your way. Any chance y'all can get together?"

A voice inside my head said, *This is perfectly harmless. You can give her one of your books. God can really use this as an opportunity for you to bear witness to your faith.*

Wonder what she meant by "y'all." Does she mean me'all or us'all or what?

**Day 63.** Tonight I reached a personal best of 67,100 points in Pac-Man, this fabulous little retro maze game. It's quite harmless, really; you just play when you have a few minutes to kill. It's a gift, this little game. It's like a late-evening walk. It relaxes me.

**Day 64.** Must admit that I find myself thinking about the East Coast novelist, a blue-eyed bombshell, even in church. Can't believe my own wickedness sometimes. I've been a follower of Jesus for a hundred years, but still seem ready to cash in my chips at the drop of a compliment.

I tried to put her out of my mind by reading my Bible during the sermon. Dared not just flip it open and start to read. What if it opened to the Song of Solomon?

Maybe if I pray for her salvation that will help. And I'll tell one of my friends she's been sending messages. And I'll block her from my Facebook page. But what if she catches wind of it and thinks I'm rude or have real problems?

**Day 66.** While having lunch with my friend Chris, I decided to be honest. I told him about the romance novelist and the dream she had about me the first time we met. He almost choked on his tuna-on-wheat, and I had forgotten how to administer the Heimlich. Thankfully, he's okay.

We talked of temptation and, though neither of us has engaged in the following activities, we pretty much agreed that these are some of the warning signs that you are sliding toward an affair:

- You send her prayer requests like, "Please pray for me as it is so difficult living with my wife. Pray that God will help me continue to be the gentle, sensitive, apprecia-tive, relational husband that I am, remembering her birthday, supporting her dreams, setting my schedule aside just to be there for her, though I remain unappre-ciated and unrewarded."
- You think about her more than twice an hour and sometimes show up at her door saying, "I found these flowers just outside. Did you drop them?"
- You see your spouse at her worst when she is tired and not so perky, and you forget that you rarely look like a first-place prize winner at the Hunk Convention yourself.
- The drug of infatuation has you asking her advice: "I know that you're a woman and can help me understand how my wife thinks. She is cranky and incommunicado. What do you think I should do?"
- You ask the Lord to gently take out each other's spouses so you can comfort each other and have a church-sanctioned marriage. Like Henry VIII.

"Promise me you'll call me before engaging in any of these behaviors," said Chris.

I promised.

**Day 67.** Today I made a list of the things I'd forfeit if ever I had
an affair:

- money
- peace
- joy
- really good, home-cooked meals every day
- my wife's trust
- my trust
- walking my daughter down the aisle with people
  crying for all the right reasons
- credibility with my sons
- my ministry
- friends trusting me around their wives
- being able to look everyone I meet straight in the eye
- guilt-free family reunions
- staring at the ceiling late at night when everyone's
  asleep and grinning like a carefree little kid

**Day 68.** 9 p.m. Chris called, saying, "I will personally murder
you if you don't remove her from your Facebook friends list right
now while I hold the line." Sometimes he's my friend, and sometimes
he's my conscience.

"Already did. Last night."

"How are you doing with lust?"

"Um…I could use some prayer."

9:05 p.m. I came up with a list of the benefits of having an
affair:

1. Temporary pleasure

I called Chris and read him my list. Then I asked him, "Can you
think of anything else?"

He couldn't.

I compared today's list with yesterday's. Hmm.

Then I quickly tore up both lists, lest my wife finds them and calls our pastor for counseling.

10:22 p.m. I told Ramona how wicked I am; how I need forgiveness and accountability and lots and lots of love. And how I will vacuum the carpets and cut the grass. It's nice to hear laughter in our home again.

**Day 69.** When I was small I thought a fibula was a small lie.

I realized today that one of the earliest lies I ever believed was that if I gave myself to God, he would make me miserable—have me marry the homeliest girl in class and spend my life playing flute in a marching band. In the Creation story, the snake tried it on Eve and she fell for it. But the truth is this: We are wired to find our delight in God alone. His commands aren't joy killers; they are for our protection and our pleasure.

**Day 70.** While mowing the lawn, I started singing an old hymn at the top of my lungs. I jazzed it up a little to match the syncopated misfiring cadence of the pitiful lawn mower engine. I'm pretty sure neighbors can hear me singing, but who cares? I am ecstatic. Praising God for the smell of the grass, the blue in the sky, the zip in my marriage, the spring in my step.

Cutting grass is the closest I've come to prolonged prayer lately. But suddenly, while trying to pray, I am entertaining a procession of negative events from my life. It's like a homecoming parade that lasts three weeks. Rolling slowly past are self-accusations, regrets, things I thought I'd settled long ago. I considered stopping the lawn mower to get on my knees and repent, but what if a neighbor were to see me? I guess I could pretend to be picking up tiny shards of glass or something that's radioactive.

Then there's this other thing that's really toasting my waffles. A guy I thought was a close friend has dumped me. It's like reliving the train-wreck ending of a high school romance. Though it happened weeks ago, I'm still stewing about it. I did talk with him, but it went nowhere.

Today I see his face on the dandelions and take great delight in lopping them off.

**Day 71.** I've been timing our pastor. So far it's a forty-seven-minute talk from Ephesians. Someone told me years ago not to take my watch to church unless I'm speaking. He said it's a distraction, and he was right. So I started leaving mine at home each week, and now I have to look at my wife's watch. It's right there on her arm.

How honest should a person be when in church? Do I tell the pastor that the sermon was great, but it was like a pie, it needed some shortening? Do I shake his hand and say, "Pastor, that sermon was... uh...timely"? Certainly I should stop telling Jerry Root, "I love your tie!" (Purple stripes were best before 1977.)

My son Steve was here visiting, and he asked me what I thought of the message. I told him the truth: that I was distracted by other things that I shouldn't have been thinking of, and so I started reading my Bible and next thing I knew, they were closing in prayer. "Really?" he said. "It was good."

"The music was great," I said. "I like how they incorporated so many different instruments, including the flute."

**Day 72.** I've been lying awake thinking of the friend who dumped me, who disappeared completely off my radar. He has spread false rumors and damaged my reputation. My wife says I should pray for him, but all that comes out is, "Lord, may the front wheels fall off his shopping cart. May a watermelon fall out and land on his toe."

Does this count as prayer?

**Day 73.** A letter arrives from a would-be author, asking me to endorse her book. She gets right to it.

Greetings Phil Callaway,

God told me to write you. He spoke to me on a tour bus in Fiji, "I am going to make you a best-selling author." I'm a writer of divine revelation and I need some help. God continues to overflow me with revelation that is for right now that will change lives dramatically. I keep it real and I tell the truth. Whatever God tells me to write that's what comes forth. God is speaking to my heart and this is what He says. "You need help...ask for it, the time is now! I have already assigned you help! You have to seek it! They will know instantly once you reach out! They will benefit greatly because they have been divinely assigned to help you birth My desires! These books will be appreciated by multiple men and women. Write a letter and send it out to who I tell you to!"

I saw you on TV, Phil Callaway, and knew you were the one. Time has been stolen from me and I need help to get out multiple book projects during this fruitful season of my life. God has authorized me to publish seven books over the next seven years.

Multitudes will be blessed and balanced by them. I'm expecting the supernatural! Please help.[1]

Why am I not hearing from God like she is? Am I out of sync with God's will? Have I really been assigned to birth God's desires and help make her very, very wealthy?

**Day 75.** Read a quote today: "Lying is done with words and also with silence." Saw a bumper sticker too: "Reincarnation is making a comeback."

**Day 76.** Told a friend that his car is nicer than mine. This was hard for me—like playing the oboe with mittens. But it's true. And a little liberating. Wish he would have said, "Nah. You have a fine car."

**Day 77.** I write to Would-Be Author and, at first, hide behind my busy schedule. Then I think, *No, I need to be honest.* So I type this: "I'm sorry, God has not spoken to me about getting involved. I wish you all the best."

**Day 78.** No one can doubt the sincerity of our church's worship leader. This morning he led us in a rousing version of "I Could Sing of Your Love Forever," then commenced to sing it over and over with his eyes closed, causing some to wonder if he was taking the song literally. Would we find him there, in the same stance, next Sunday?

Finally he moved on to a different song. But he made the mistake of stopping after the first stanza to gently chide us for not lifting up our hands. (It was a song about standing to lift up our hands.)

Many obliged, a few quite enthusiastically, though most of us just turned our hands over and held them beside our hips rather awkwardly, like we were in a showdown in an old Western, waiting for someone to yell, "Draw!"

Just before mealtime, my son Steve asked what I thought of the service. "The service here is excellent," I told him. "Your mother serves us so well. I am just so thankful. Let us pray."

**Day 79.** In just four days, it's our anniversary. I don't mean to boast, but every single year since 1982 I have remembered.

**Day 80.** No, strike that. There was that time in 1993 when I completely forgot. For the most part, though, I remember well but don't plan big. I envy guys who stage romantic anniversary getaways, exotic cruises, or walks through forests where trees light up and music plays and little kids in leprechaun suits jump out and dance. No, let me be honest. These guys make me physically ill.

But this year I think Ramona will like what I've planned, if I can keep it a secret.

**Day 82.** I lied today, but in a purposeful sort of way.

Ramona asked what we will be doing for our anniversary. I said, "I'll cook something."

She didn't exactly do cartwheels at the prospect, just said, "Um, that's it?"

"Yes."

"But I heard you talking with Kevin and Ivy on the phone. Are we going somewhere with them?"

I wanted to save the celebration as a surprise, so I said, "No, I asked if they could, but they can't. They're sorry. They wanted me to wish you a happy anniversary. It's a super busy time for them with school starting and all."

Why did I need to tell five lies when I could have stopped at one? It's like I'd gone without chocolate for a year and was eating it by the fistful.

Ramona said, "But they homeschool."

"They do? That's right. I'd forgotten," I lie, shutting the door behind me and heading for the backyard.

I thought of an example from Scripture of a lie told with purpose and God blessing the act. It was the prostitute Rahab who hid the spies and lied to Israel's enemies who were looking for them.[2] She even landed in the Hall of Faith (see Hebrews 11 if you doubt me). My lie was rather pitiful in the grand scheme of things, and certainly no one's life was saved, but I couldn't help deluding myself with the thought that I'm in pretty good company.

**Day 83.** I'm learning that you should never tell a lie to your spouse, but you shouldn't always tell the truth either. As my dad used to say, "A closed mouth gathers no foot." I find a little acrostic that spells THINK helps:

**T**—Is what I'm about to tell her True?

**H**—Is it Helpful?

**I**—Will it Inspire her?

**N**—Is it Necessary?

**K**—Am I Kind about it?

**Day 84.** I packed a small suitcase, sneaked it into the car, then asked Ramona to go get some groceries with me. On the way to the store, we turned the wrong way and headed out of town.

She said, "Hey!"

"I just wanted to show you something."

Two hitchhikers were standing on the shoulder of the road, their thumbs out, clad in sunglasses and hats—and clothing too. I pulled over. Ramona thought I'd completely lost it. Kevin and his wife, Ivy, jumped in, and we were off for a few days of pampering.

"You know what I love about homeschooling?" I asked, knowing the joke would be met with groans.

They leaned forward.

"You can wear pajamas to school and not get kicked out."

Kevin and Ivy wonder how Ramona has stayed married to me for so long. I'm not sure either.

For the most part, ours has been a practical marriage, I told them. When I'm wrong, I admit it. When I'm right, I try my best to shut up. One of the ways my wife gets me to do stuff is to tell me that I probably can't.

Our friends find this funnier than I thought they would. Even funnier than the homeschool joke.

**Day 85.** Why can't marriage be more like today? Lazy breakfast. Riverside stroll. It's like we're a duet. When one sings, the other claps. We've been through a lot in nigh onto thirty years together. Sometimes the better comes after the worse.

Tonight I stuck a note on a bottle of expensive perfume, then left it on Ramona's pillow. The note says, "If I told you I love you, would you neck with me?"

## Honest Confession #3

I didn't want to write about lust. It's easier to appear to have it all together and leave readers with lofty thoughts of me. But this is a book on honesty.

When I was a teenager, I thought, *If I live to be forty, then this lust thing will vanish and I can live in complete victory like the forty-year-olds around here who look like they have one foot in the grave and the other on a skateboard.* Unfortunately, after more than four decades as a believer, I find there are times when I still fail in this area. I admire leaders such as George Verwer who have been blunt about their battles,[3] but few topics bring out the modern-day Pharisees in greater force than the sins of others.

When I sin, I confess immediately and give thanks that the One who called the Pharisees' bluff is on my side. First John 2:1 tells me that Christ defends me before the Father and that I am forgiven and loved. That love is not a license to sin, but it compels me to walk on with him. And I walk with a limp. So do my greatest heroes of the faith. Maybe that limp is why so many can catch up to us and ask for help.

George Verwer wrote, "I am a sinner, who's growing stronger through the years, who crawls back to the cross when he sins and finds God still loves him and will still use him to bring others to Christ. That's grace, isn't it."[4]

# FOUR

# With Friends Like These

Men are liars. We'll lie about lying if we have to.
I'm an algebra liar. I figure two good lies make
a positive.

—Tim Allen

All lies are not told—some are lived.

—Arnold Glasow

**D**ay 86. Tonight my wife caught me playing Pac-Man. She dropped a copy of John Piper's *Don't Waste Your Life* beside the computer keyboard (from about ten inches) and left the room shaking her head. I had just set a goal for myself of reaching 100,000 points. If I can do that, I will definitely quit.

Later, Ramona reentered the room and said, "Would you mind vacuuming?" It wasn't so much a question, really.

"Sure, but um…um…"

"The phrase you're groping for is, 'Yes, dear.'" I think she read this on a fridge magnet.

"I'm having fun," I said. "This game sure relaxes me."

She left the room muttering something about dust bunnies, but I couldn't make it out.

"I'll vacuum in half an hour," I hollered. "Promise." I was up to 73,000 points and had two lives left.

Ramona poked her head around the corner and said, "I'm nagging you because I love you."

I snorted. Then she started to laugh.

This laughter has kept us married a hundred and fifty years. I lost both Pac lives, laughing, and forgot all about the vacuuming.

**Day 87.** Ramona provided the answer to my Day 85 question: "Yes."

**Day 88.** Gord Allert, a friend who works at a funeral home, called today with an irresistible invitation. But first I asked: "How's business?"

He's impervious to funeral-home jokes. Whenever I introduce him to new acquaintances, they seem to always have a graveyard joke ready. ("Everyone's dying to get into your cemetery.") Gord seems to be listening, but really he's sizing them up, knowing that everyone he meets is a potential client.

Today we talked of how divorce, drug abuse, and suicide are running wild in his line of work. I ask how he gets through. "God," he said, "and golf." Then he asked me to join him at the annual Western District Funeral Home Tournament.

"Our team stinks," he admitted. "Even you could help us win."

"What's the prize?" I asked. "A free cremation?" This isn't funny to Gord.

"We'll fly you to Oregon if you can make the date work. It's October first."

"Um...let me see, free golf?"

"Ya."

"Meals?"

"Yup."

"All the expenses?"

"Uh-huh."

"First class?"

"Not a chance."

"Okay, I feel complete peace about it. I'm dying to play. Who will I be golfing with?"

"Friends of mine who drink like fish, smoke like chimneys, and cheat like Vegas."

"On second thought, maybe I should stay home and—"

"You already said yes. And remember, you're writing a book about honesty."

"Of corpse, of corpse."

**Day 89.** I have been genuinely and repeatedly wronged by this so-called friend who dumped me, badly enough to have to forgive him every waking hour. Actually, I tell myself I forgive him, but I don't. I stew in my anger. I lie awake thinking of what to do about his unjustified actions. I have considered

1. writing him a letter;
2. writing letters to the local newspaper;
3. distributing leaflets on street corners;
4. mentioning a prayer request in church during the sharing time;
5. maybe placing a defense of my noble character in the church bulletin.

I know I'm supposed to pray for my enemies, but it doesn't say how often. I will pray for him twice in the coming year.

I will begin with the following prayer:

Dear God, I need you to kill someone for me. It will be the perfect crime. If you do it, I can get away with it. Perhaps this sounds harsh to you, but consider my side of the story. This guy has gossiped about me, written me anonymous letters (I know they are from him, because I know his handwriting), and fabricated stuff you wouldn't believe. So go ahead and make my year. Make it look accidental. He drives a motorcycle, and I was thinking, *What if the front wheel just flew off on one of those mountain curves?* Better yet, something catastrophic would be nice. A building collapsing. A cement truck unloading through his sunroof. I know I'm supposed to love my enemies, but I'm having a little trouble, Lord. Help![1]

**Day 90.** I'm still stewing. Is it time to retract my vindictive prayer?

**Day 91.** My friend Regi called today and wants to have lunch early next week. You don't suppose he would ask about the ——. Naw.

**Day 92.** There was a five- or six-member worship band at church today, depending on whether you counted the kid flipping sheet music for his mother at the Roland keyboard. The music was an eclectic mix, designed to make everyone happy. One from the Singopiration sixties ("I'll Fly Away"), one from the Maranatha! eighties ("As the Deer"), a few from the ensuing decades, and a meaty Charles Wesley hymn to close things out ("And Can It Be").

Our eighteenish-year-old electric guitarist knows only one style—that of using the Deep Purple/Boz Skaggs fuzz box. He distorts everything and loves to hold out the last note for all it's worth—a full eight counts after the others have stopped playing. Some of the older folk had not previously been treated to this particular arrangement of "A Mighty Fortress Is Our God," and they don't mind saying so.

Ernest Winkler, who looks like he had a side order of prunes for breakfast, shook my hand in the foyer and said, "I haven't heard louder noise in years."

"I kind of liked it," I said.

I was smiling, feeling quite jovial as I left church.

**Day 93.** I confided to my wise friend James that I've been calling heavenly brimstone down on someone who had wronged me. He smiled and told me the story of a chaplain who was comforting a dying man. In the final stages of cancer, the man confessed that he'd spent the night ranting and raving against God. So much so, that he wondered how God could forgive him and if his chance of eternal life had vanished.

The chaplain asked, "What do you think is the opposite of love?"

"Hate," said the dying man.

The chaplain replied, "No, the opposite of love is indifference. You have not been indifferent with God or you would never have spent the night honestly telling him what was in your heart. Do you know the Christian word that describes what you have been doing? The word is *prayer*. You spent the night praying."

**Day 95.** Can't believe I spent thirty-five minutes playing a stupid game you can't win! I tell myself that Pac-Man is a complete waste of time. Never again! That's it. Put a fork in me and call me done. I quit!

**Day 96.** Today I'm at a conference with a few fellow authors who are trying to sell their wares. I compliment one of them on a book he's written. "God wrote it really," he says.

I'm surprised by my response. "No he didn't. I've read his material. It's better than this."

I do this with a grin, and he returns a sheepish smile. Did I just say that? This truth experiment is really getting to me.

**Day 97.** Met with Regi for coffee, still wondering why he wanted to get together. I can't stand coffee and always settle for tea, but I knew it was time to get things out in the open, head things off at the pass, nip them in the bud.

"Reg," I spluttered, as he took a pull at his mocha java cappusomething, "I cheated. I did. I haven't done this often, but there was no way I was going to let you and Vance beat Harold and me at golf. It's a game I cannot abide losing, but I'm sorry."

He set down the cup, and I watched his grin turn to a chuckle, then blossom into a full-fledged laugh.

"I'd forgotten all about that. You cheated?"

"I did. I'm sorry. Was there anything else you'd like to know about me?"

"Oh yes, but I really just wanted to see how you were doing." He started to laugh again. "You cheated? You cheated!"

Phew. He was so delighted by my confession that he seemed oblivious to the other item I thought he'd bring up.

**Day 98.** I asked my social networking friends for some golf tips, then added one of my own. "Lathering your opponent's grips with Vaseline gives you a six-stroke advantage heading into the second hole." I've spent much of the last three months saying, "Just kidding."

**Day 99.** I spoke at a church today, far from home. The first person I met was the greeter. He pulled me aside, poked his finger in my face, and said, "Why don't you dress up for God?" My first thought was, *He's joking.* But he wasn't. Funny thing is, I was dressed quite nicely. Even had a tie on; a rare occurrence for me. My inquisitor knew I was the morning's speaker and informed me that the Old Testament priests took care with their clothing, unlike me.

I couldn't resist. "Should I wear a breastplate?" I asked.

That didn't help.

"You don't even have a suit coat!" he groaned.

Was this an impractical joke? I tried to carefront him, but the right words wouldn't come.

Later, the pastor apologized profusely. "He's our greeter," he said. "It's his last time."

I know I'll hear a hundred positive comments this month. But which comment do you suppose I'll remember?

**Day 100.** On the flight home, I watched a movie. The title, *The Invention of Lying,* intrigued me for obvious reasons. The film explores what the world would be like if there were no such thing as deceitful, falsehood-spouting fibbers. In other words, if everyone on earth took a truth vow like mine and stuck to it. Sadly, the movie skewers my faith, so I decided to read a book instead, but not before smiling through the most honest ad for Coca-Cola you'll ever see: "Coke's very high in sugar, and like any high-calorie soda, it leads to obesity in children and adults. But I'm Bob. I work for Coke. I'm asking you to not stop buying Coke." Pepsi ads on buses say, "For when they don't have Coke."[2]

I wonder what the world would be like if more churches posted honest signs:

OUR GREETERS AREN'T THE FRIENDLIEST,

BUT YOU'LL LOVE OUR POTLUCK.

COME HEAR OUR PASTOR.

HE'S NOT THAT GREAT, BUT HE'S SHORT.

**Day 102.** I told my younger son about the confrontational church greeter and asked if, when he pictures Christians, he thinks of cranky people. "Nah," he said, smiling. "We've had too much fun around here."

**Day 103.** I usually come up with clever responses to criticism three days after the event. Today I had an imaginary conversation with the gentleman who dressed me down for not dressing up.

"I spent much of my life trying to dress up for God," I found myself saying to the couch. "Then I discovered that my righteousness is as filthy as rags." My timing isn't great, but the truth is there.[3]

**Day 106.** Very little that I would be proud to report occurred this past week. Plenty of stewing on the menu, a little whining, some unforgiveness, the odd doubt, and a side order of ingratitude. Just being honest.

So today I sat in church wondering, *Is there hope for me?*

**Day 107.** A question arrived from Andy, an acquaintance who calls himself agnostic. "Every year a million people are trafficked across borders and sold into sexual slavery to be horribly abused. Most are women and kids. What does your faith say to them?"

I do know what my faith doesn't say to them. It doesn't deny the existence of pain—as Christian Science does. It doesn't say there is no personal God and these things are an inevitable part of fate—as Buddhism does. It doesn't say that suffering in this life is because of behavior in a previous life, so just endure it well so you'll attain a better ranking in your next reincarnation—as Hinduism does. But my answer could occupy an entire book. Shoot. I'll have to think a little harder before responding.

**Day 108.** I spoke to a roomful of nurses who smoke and drink and swear and like to laugh at my clean jokes. No one chewed me out for not wearing a breastplate. Do I sound bitter?

**Day 111.** Nothing much happened all day. Honest. Hardly a thing to report.

**Day 113.** Lighthearted questions are still trickling in from friends who have taken a liking to my truth vow. Meryl asked if I have ever fudged my score on the golf course. "I don't play very often," she wrote, "but I am amazed at how easily people skip entering those really bad shots!"

Funny she should mention this. I'm off to Oregon to play in a tournament in a few days. Most nights, my wife and I pray together out loud before drifting off to sleep. Tonight I prayed, "Lord, help me not cheat." Ramona flipped on the light and just lay there, glaring at me with her left eye above the sheets.

**Day 115.** Jesus was a friend of sinners, according to my mother and even the accusatory Pharisees, as recorded in the gospels of Matthew and Luke. But while I'm being honest, I'd better admit that there's little evidence to convict me of the same crime. Mostly, I hang out with churched people who were born and raised in the Psalms and Proverbs. They get jokes about Rebecca being the first smoker in the Bible because she lit up on her camel, and Elijah's parents being smart businesspeople because they made a little prophet.

I once went an entire week without talking to a nonbeliever, smelling cigar smoke, or hearing a cuss word. Then my brother—a Baptist minister—arrived and all that changed. Truth is, I'm more comfortable viewing pagans from a distance, like fifth-grade boys who huddle together at recess talking about talking to girls.

Tomorrow, however, I am being flown to Portland, Oregon, to hang out with real live sinners—funeral-home people who want me on their golf foursome because they've been getting soundly whomped and think I can help stop the bleeding. They're grasping at straws. My golf game has been borderline catastrophic of late, and I bet these guys will rip my head off if I don't score well. I wonder if I'm a Chihuahua with its tongue out the window, unaware that he's traveling to a pit bull convention.

Before crawling into bed, I asked my wife for advice on which golf shirt to wear. I have three—all of them gifts—each with a slogan on it:

Promise Keepers: Manhood… Let the Truth Be Told

Bethany Bible Church: "I Can Do All Things Through Christ Which Strengtheneth Me" (Phil 4:13)

## I MADE A
*triple bogey on every*

## HOLE
*I even threw my putter*

## IN ONE
*of the stupid lakes*

"Hmm," Ramona said. "That's a tough one."

## Honest Confession #4

Andy the agnostic's question has troubled me since Day 107. Partly because I get so self-centered and forget those who have real-world adversity. What would I say to those dear women and children who have been sold into slavery?

In my feeble response, I told Andy that my son has been in Uganda, serving among people sold into slavery, offering food and a hope that I believe Jesus alone can offer. I told him about David and Beth Grant, who work with women sold to the brothels of Mumbai. They have established Homes for Hope so those trapped in prostitution can find safety, receive an education, and recover their dignity. Yes, they are unapologetically Christian about it, but if you compare the success rate of their organization with those who are spiritually neutral, you'll be astonished. Beth said, "What a difference Jesus makes. For you and I? Yes. But for millions of women and children in the world who are literally in hell, the promises of God are just as real and relevant.... They are powerful. For those who turn their face toward him, he brings change and new life."[4]

The believers I admire don't sit around guessing at God's role as much as they follow the One who told a story about the Good Samaritan, a person who went out of his way to reach out to a beaten, abused man who was his religious and ethnic adversary. I need to be more like them.

# FIVE

# A Wretch Like Me

A half truth is a whole lie.

—YIDDISH PROVERB

The truth will set you free, but first it will
make you miserable.

—JAMES A. GARFIELD

**Day 116.** Looking out the window from seat 12A, I saw Mount
Baker rise like a blueberry sundae surrounded by whipped clouds.
All it needed was a cherry. I gazed at it while I wondered about the
friend-of-sinners thing. How truthful was Jesus when he talked with
pagans over a meal? Did they laugh at his jokes? Did he laugh at
theirs? Was he the designated driver?

Camas Meadows is a deceiving name for a golf course, on account of the fact that it has no meadows. All I found there were
pencil-thin fairways guarded by tall trees. The brochure promised
meadows with "a beautiful array of Camas Lilies" plus "the largest
known patch of Bradshaw's Lomatium," an endangered perennial
herb. (Is this an oxymoron?) After three holes, I was still looking for

them. For me, the course consisted of tiny patches of slippery grass and vast sand bunkers, the envy of the Sahara.

Today I shared a cart with Larry, a well-mannered thirty-year-old who looks like John Daly after a stint with the South Beach Diet. Larry's nerves were jangling at the start as he hacked his way through the woods yelling, "Timber!" Whenever he got the chance, he downed a can of Heineken. "I'm sorry I'm drinking so much," he muttered, "but it relaxes me." And he was right. The more he drank, the better he played.

"Wow," I said, after Larry uncorked his seventh or eighth brew. "Don't they sell that in kegs?" "I'm used to stronger beer," he said. "This stuff couldn't get a squirrel tipsy."

"I better drive the cart," I offered.

The others in our foursome had mixed opinions on guzzling and golf. One called beer "swing lube." Another had learned the hard way, saying, "Four beers and bad things happen to me." (Without beer, he hits about a foot behind the ball when he swings. With beer, he can't see the ball and needs someone else to tee it up.) One thing they all agreed on: people consume less when there's betting involved.

We headed for the woods to search for Larry's ball, and he turned the discussion to me: "Hey, aren't you a minister or something?"

"Uh…well, I write books about faith, does that count?"

"I knew a Christian once," he said. "He was one ——," and I shan't quote the rest. Trust me when I say it was not a compliment.

"Are you married?" I asked him.

"Sort of, but not really. We've been living together ten years. Just keep putting it off, I guess."

"What hindereth ye from taking unto you this woman as thy lawfully wedded wife?"

He laughed. "Sometime maybe."

"Where is she? We can do this thing today."

He was grinning widely. "Know something? If you had a church, I'd go. You can be my preacher anytime."

■ ■ ■

Dinner was served at Salty's, with its sweeping view of the Columbia River. There were seven of us, and since Larry had unmasked me as a quasi-minister, they were confessing things to me in rapid succession. It's like they thought I was their priest.

They asked questions: Where's your clerical collar? Do you believe in hell and the Bible and the Resurrection and all that stuff? Are you a rabbi?

Larry asked in all seriousness, "Can you do circumcisions?"

"You bet I can. But I'm just learning. Any volunteers?"

Our mountain of seafood arrived, and I raised my hand. "If I'm the minister, I get to ask the blessing." Everyone bowed his head.

"Lord, in a world where so many are hungry, we thank you for food. Where so many are lonely, we thank you for friends. Where so many live without hope, we thank you for your Son, Jesus Christ. Amen."

They couldn't stop thanking me.

I didn't push anything on them, but when they asked, I talked a little about my faith. Mostly, though, we laughed together. And back at the hotel, I gave each of them a copy of a golf book I wrote.

Several offered me big, manly hugs, and I'd like to think it had nothing to do with the vats of alcohol they had consumed.

I offered up a prayer as the elevator doors opened. "Lord, I hope I didn't get in the way of them seeing you."

**Day 119.** Regi called today and asked, "Did you sign me up for Peter Popoff's newsletter?"

"Peter who?"

"You know, the late-night preacher who heals everybody. I got some miracle spring water in the mail. We've had eleven letters from this guy."

"Really."

He laughed. "Do you know who did it?"

"I did it, Reg. I can't believe it took you this long to ask."

**Day 120.** I can't help reflecting on my golf trip and, with it being Sunday today, I shall tell the unvarnished truth. I am normally a nice, amiable man who attempts to follow Jesus, but the sporting world knocks the stuffing out of me. It tempts and coaxes me to spit, kick, and swear. Golf is the worst. There is hardly a moment on a golf course anywhere that I do not consider some form of cheating.

On Day 116, I fought it valiantly until the thirteenth hole. This is a hole where the green is four hundred yards in front of you, and million-dollar homes line up like debutantes just forty yards to your left. I shanked a ball westward, but the hole lies to the north. Trudging into the trees, I found a ball lying there. Were it not for my wretched truth vow, I can almost guarantee I would have kicked it from behind a tree while pointing at cloud formations. But I kept looking.

Thankfully, I found the prodigal ball, a Titleist Pro V1. From my bag I yanked a six-iron and hit the stupid thing toward the green, from whence I heard the noises of a man excited. At first I thought I'd hit him. But he was hollering the kind of holler you holler when you have won a dishwasher on *The Price Is Right*. I had a hole in two!

I removed the ball from the cup, kissed it, and thanked the imaginary audience. But as I teed it up for my first shot on the following hole, I noted that it had no red stripe on it, a striking difference from the one I'd been hitting.

What to do?

I looked back toward the fairway. No one was looking for a ball. Perhaps my eyes were deceiving me. Perhaps I had hit it so hard the identifying mark had vanished. At times I have hit golf balls so hard and so far into grass so tall that the logo changed, so anything is possible. And then there is the matter of my getting older. Perhaps I was confused about the ball having a red stripe. I was able to convince myself that golf is a horribly unfair game played by people whose shorts are too tight. I concluded that I had indeed hit an amazing shot and should be rewarded.

Now it's Sunday night and I'm lying in bed. All I can think about is the ball I drove into the cup. Me, the foursome's honorary minister. A guy who very likely might be called upon to perform a circumcision. A guy who can pray well enough to elicit manly hugs afterward.

A dyed-in-the-wool cheater.

**Day 122.** Great response from Chuck Rogers, a childhood friend turned lawyer whom I ripped off a hundred years ago. He wants no repayment, just my promise that if I'm ever in the area, I'll stop by and see his family and call him Charles. Ah, to seek the forgiveness of a lawyer and find it! God is good.

**Day 123.** I was so overwhelmed by this newfound sense of forgiveness that I called my guzzling golf partner, Larry, to tell him of my woeful cheating on the golf course.

"Hey, I need a priest," I said. "Do you know one?"

"What?"

"I need to confess something."

"You do?"

"Yep." And I told him everything.

Larry said, "I wasn't going to read your book, but now I will. You're human. I kinda like that."

Hardly the response I'd been expecting. Do you suppose we'd be forgiven more if we asked more often?

**Day 124.** Having been hanging out with pagans at the golf tournament and hearing their questions has me wanting to find reasonable answers. An idea hit me: I could take the time I spend playing Pac-Man to study up on apologetics.

That can be my reward if I reach 100,000 points.

**Day 126.** Today my college-student son Jeff brought a friend over. And his friend's brother. These guys are like locusts. Nice locusts, kind locusts, but hungry ones. They plunder and loot our pantry, and we love them. When the friends' parents moved to a different city, the guys stayed in town to live with their older brother. But Jeff's friend Paul misses his mother's cooking, judging from the way he shows up at our house whenever our oven door opens.

We love Paul, but he has a disgusting habit. He likes to cram cigarettes in his mouth and light them on fire. Unlike a certain U.S. president, he inhales.

I've told him he is welcome to smoke inside our house just as soon as I am free to discharge firearms in his. So he doesn't smoke here. He goes on long walks instead.

I must show patience with Paul when he comes into the house smelling like Philip Morris. Tonight we talk about other habits that are far more damaging: like gossip and slander and greed and disobedience. He's a nice kid. I wonder what I could do to help him quit.

**Day 127.** A skeptical friend asked me, "While you're being so honest, tell me why you go to church."

I'll think of other answers later on, but today I mentioned the guy who lifts his hands the highest in our church. He's the one with the least reason to do so. Kevin Penner and his wife, Laurel, spent years studying the Mixtec language in Mexico so they could translate the Bible. Genesis was 20 percent complete when the unthinkable happened. Due to complications and some primitive medicine, their baby suffered a severe brain injury during delivery. A zillion dollars later, they are back home with a child who can do nothing but stare through vacant eyes, with no hope of ever uttering a single word.

Kevin is a golfing buddy, and we've talked about disappointment and the sovereignty of God. He has more questions than answers, but there he was this morning, lifting his hands skyward as we sang "How Great Is Our God."

It's the most profound sermon I will hear this week.

**Day 130.** I finally managed to hit 100,000 points in Pac-Man! I shut the computer down and picked up a book. Such discipline.

I should probably pick up a vacuum too.

**Day 131.** One of the advantages of writing for magazines is that I can interview well-known Christians and ask them questions on behalf of my readers. In a couple of weeks I'm scheduled to talk with Chuck Colson, the feisty lawyer who climbed the career ladder to become Richard Nixon's hatchet man.

He was indicted in the Watergate scandal that brought down the presidency, and then he was locked in prison. I began reading his books when I was a teenager. Maybe I can ask him some apologetics questions so I won't have to read so much.

**Day 134.** An elderly gentleman called tonight to apologize for his extreme anger toward me when I cut him off in the church parking lot this morning. Said he wanted to honk at me, but had settled for pounding his fists on the steering wheel and "saying some unChristlike things." God convicted him and he knew he was to call me and "keep short accounts."

There is a slight problem. I wasn't in town at the time of the infraction. I was speaking in a church far away and had just arrived home before the phone rang. I have a multitude of witnesses.

In light of my vow of truth, I mentioned this to him. He insisted, "No. It was you. I know your car."

He described a station wagon, a type of vehicle that I have not owned (nor driven even five feet) in my entire life. I now face an ethical dilemma on numerous fronts, most notably this: Is it possible to forgive someone on behalf of the actual person who aroused the anger, when you do not know who that person is? And if I do not forgive the elderly caller, will I be able to forgive myself for the damage I will undoubtedly do by suggesting (even indirectly) that he is senile?

I thought about it while he talked and finally said, "Of course I forgive you, my brother." An audible sigh escaped his lips, a sigh of the forgiven.

*Is God happy with me for lying?* I wonder. In the history of lies, this may be among the most guileless ever committed, and possibly one of the most productive.

**Day 136.** Wesley M, a distant acquaintance, confided that he has been unable to attract a wife the conventional way, so he sought my wise advice. I have no idea why I did this, but I suggested he join an online Christian dating service. What can it hurt?

**Day 138.** Our Maltese Shih Tzu has a nice temperament, unless something moves. Tonight she took off after a dear lady with whom I've been trying to share my faith. Mojo scared the poor girl to death. Hope she doesn't think this is part of my witnessing strategy.

**Day 140.** I picked out a fridge magnet for my wife. It says, "No husband has ever been shot while doing the dishes." It's quite a hit.

After dinner, my neighbor Jackson came by to tell us his six-year-old daughter was missing. "She said she was running away from home," he said. That was two hours earlier. I called four friends, and an hour later half the town was looking for the girl. A few said they preferred to stay home and pray. They felt they could be of greater help that way.

Arlen and I prayed a little, but mostly, as darkness descended, we shined our dying flashlights in the most ridiculous places. A cell phone rang. The girl had been found hiding under some thick branches.

Arlen looked at his watch. "I better go watch my favorite show."

"What is it?"

"*Lost.*"

**Day 141.** I love this church. There's something here for everyone. We rotate worship teams so you never quite know what's coming. Country, emo, contemporary, hymns. It ensures that every Sunday a different interest group will be offended.

**Day 142.** I called Chuck Colson and told him about my experiment to go a year without a lie. Then I confided that I've not always
had an easy time confronting others when I need to.

"Too many of us live life fearful of offending others," he said.
"The trouble with living this way is that we never have the joy of
knowing we've contributed to the transformation of someone's life. I
first heard the claims of Jesus because a nervous friend talked to me
and gave me a book."

"Speaking of books," I said, "I've been reading one by antitheist
Richard Dawkins that calls into question everything I've ever been
taught about faith. He says Christianity has made nothing but negative contributions to human history."

"That's absurd," said Colson. "Richard Dawkins considers religious instruction a form of child abuse and calls on governments to
stop it. He accuses us of wanting a government run by the church.
That runs contrary to the most basic Christian teaching about free
will and human freedom."

I started wishing I could think and talk like Colson. But I didn't
tell him that. Instead, I tried to sound intelligent, inserting the odd
"um" so he couldn't tell I was reading the questions.

"Christianity gave the very idea of separation of church and state
to the West," he continued. "Christianity doesn't advance by power
or conquest, but by love. Furthermore, the orthodox faith is the one
source that can renew culture. We've seen this throughout history. In
fact, you can match the rise and decline of society with the rise and
decline of Christianity."

I switched topics to something else that had been on my mind:
"How can I know that the Bible is reliable?"

"Well," said Colson, "it was assembled over four centuries of the most painstaking study, open debate, and research. Our Bible is the most studiously examined proclamation of faith ever compiled. Before the end of the 1950s, 25,000 biblical sites had been substantiated by archaeological discoveries; not one proved the Bible false. No other religious document is so accurate."

"What about *The Book of Mormon?*"

He laughed. "It talks about a civilization in North America in 400–600 BC. Not a single artifact has ever been found to substantiate it. On the other hand, thousands have been willing to lay down their lives for the Bible. It has had an unparalleled impact on countless lives over thousands of years. What has become of the teachings of the Beatles' guru, Maharishi Mahesh Yogi, or Timothy Leary's pal Baba Ram Dass? Few know what they taught anymore. But the message of the Bible continues to transform lives.

"If the Bible is evil, as antitheists charge, why has it been the bedrock of forming the most humane civilization in history? How does it continue to turn hardened criminals into gentle lambs as I have seen throughout the world? The most violent prison in Latin America is in Medellin, Colombia. It averaged one murder a day. Since Prison Fellowship took hold and the gospel came in, it now averages one murder a year."

"But what about Jesus' resurrection?" I asked. "The atheists say it was a hoax. That the disciples had a pact."

Chuck laughed. "My personal experience in the Watergate scandal convinces me of the historic proof of the Resurrection. The most powerful men around the president could not keep a lie for three weeks. And you'd have me believe that twelve apostles literally gave their lives for a lie? Impossible. As we are seeing with Islamic radicals today, people will die for something they believe to be true; but men will never die for something they know to be false."[1]

I bet Chuck Colson didn't get this smart playing Pac-Man.

**Day 143.** A boy called to talk with my daughter. I said, "Your call could be monitored by our customer service department." He laughed, so there's hope for him.

**Day 144.** More "cheetahs" are chasing me. A letter arrived from Lee: "Jesus said that if we look on a woman to lust after her, we have committed adultery in our hearts. How many of the Ten Commandments have you broken or bent?"

"Ah, Lee… Jesus said if we hate someone, we are guilty of murder, so it's not looking good for me. I have dishonored my parents and taken the Lord's name in vain. At best, I'm a work in progress. Without God's grace, I'm toast, slightly burnt, hold the butter."

## Honest Confession #5

I've always had trouble with the concept of witnessing, of sharing my faith with others. This is mostly because, for most of my life, it scared me out of my mind. I was taught that pagans were slippery, whiskey-swirling back-stabbers, who—if we could just get them saved—would turn into kind, honest, loving, churchgoing citizens by Wednesday.

It turns out, that was inaccurate.

I have discovered that all my nonbelieving friends and neighbors are made in the image of God, and many live exemplary, moral lives, sometimes putting me to shame. Maybe they believe that in doing so, they will be okay in the afterlife (assuming there is one). The Bible teaches that through Jesus' life and death, we are forgiven. It has nothing to do with our performance and everything to do with accepting the Savior.

I am not accepted because I'm so wonderful, but because he is. Thank goodness. I mean, thank God.

# SIX

# Looking for a Sign

A lie with a purpose is one of the worst kind, and the most profitable.

— FINLEY PETER DUNNE

A lie gets halfway around the world before the truth has a chance to get its pants on.

—WINSTON CHURCHILL

**D**ay 147. Have been wondering what to get my wife for her birthday. She turns, well, older in a few weeks. What do you get for a woman who already has me? So I posed this question to her: "Honey, I am such a blessing to you. Isn't that enough?" She muttered something indecipherable, except for the word "vacuum," and kept peeling potatoes.

Surely she doesn't want another vacuum? The one we have works perfectly well, last I checked.

I helped peel potatoes, and she seemed to like that.

Later, I switched to Plan B and asked my social networking friends for ideas. The women had lots of suggestions:

- a manicure
- a facial
- a pedicure
- roses
- a snuggly bathrobe
- a massage
- a day without cooking
- a weekend spa—alone
- a jigsaw puzzle made of one of her favorite pictures
- flowers on the dining-room table, along with a nice meal prepared by me (not forgetting candles and mood music)
- a poem (written by me, straight from the heart)
- make it a birthday month (by putting a different gift in a basket every day of the month leading up to her birthday)

If I am to comply, I will have to quit my job.

10 p.m. Ramona asked about my grin. I told her that for the first time in a while, I was looking forward to church tomorrow.

She seemed a little confused.

**Day 148.** Ramona wondered why I was in such a hurry to get to church this morning. "It's just the right thing to do," I contended. "We arrive early for sporting events, why not church?"

She was delighted that I had turned over a new leaf. "It's the first time we've been early since our children were baptized," she enthused, clutching her Bible, checking my speedometer, wondering if I should see a doctor.

When we arrived, I tried not to let her notice that I was scanning the parking lot, looking for station wagons.

Nothing. Not a single one.

**Day 149.** Tonight I reached 107,830 points in Pac-Man! Surely 150,000 is attainable.

Once I reach that pinnacle, it's over for me. Really. I can stop whenever I want to.

When I do, I will vacuum, then maybe reread Richard Foster's excellent book *Celebration of Discipline*.

**Day 150.** I placed a hand-lettered sign on the front lawn: WARN-ING: HIGHLY ALARMED SHIH TZU.

We got this dog for companionship, but Mojo is really a wit-nessing tool waiting to happen. You can take her on a walk and you'll strike up conversations with complete strangers in less than a minute.

"What's her name?"

"Mojo. It's a Bible name, really. Named after Moses, who stut-tered, and Jonah, who ran away. Do you have a Bible?"

I've thought of trying this, but haven't yet. I think it could work, though.

My son uses the dog as a dating tool. Take this dog out in public and you'll have six to eight college girls saying, "Aaaah cute!" before you can say, "Shih Tzu."

**Day 151.** Paul's ability to smoke is on the increase. He shows a lack of enthusiasm for many things, but in Smoking Class I give him an A+. He shows potential for three packs a day by the age of twenty.

Smoking took up Paul when he was very young. He may have asked for one in the delivery room, for all I know. Older kids thought it was cute to buy cigarettes for him, and now he's inhaling thirty a day, sometimes more if work isn't going well. He longs to quit; longs to pitch them in the furnace and run. But the habit is stickier than that.

Tonight I told him I'm praying for him—that he will run out of money before he runs out of lungs. And then I opened my mouth and said way too much. Blame it on my truth project.

I said, "Smokers are modern-day lepers. They huddle together in tiny colonies outside buildings, shivering in the cold like survivors of a nuclear meltdown. What part of this appeals to you?"

I said, "Have you ever seen an ad that states: 'Single female seeking Christian guy who smokes at least a pack a day. Hope to spend declining years nursing you through halitosis and heart disease'?"

I couldn't stop. "You are inhaling more than four thousand chemicals, including carbon monoxide and cyanide, toppings we don't put on our sundaes. Your life expectancy is that of a Bob Dylan guitar string. You are burning up $5,600 a year so you can smell like stinkweed and die early."

That was of no help whatsoever. Surely there's something else I can do.

**Day 152.** My daughter sent an e-mail: "How are you doing?" I responded, "We're fine. A little lonely in this empty nest. We sit with the dog by the window now. Mom on one side and me on the other. We prop our elbows on the back of the couch and watch passing cars, hoping. Sometimes we doze off and awake when there's a noise. Your mother barked once yesterday. But we're okay. No need to feel sorry for us, no ma'am.

"Yes there is! When are you coming home?"

"For Mom's birthday," she said.

Ah, children. What would we be without them? Rich?

■ ■ ■

I was picking out a birthday card for my wife when a pleasant voice came over the supermarket intercom: "Would the owner of a silver Camry, license plate ———, come to customer service please?"

A fellow shopper witnessed a hit and run in the parking lot. Some idiot smunched my passenger-side panel. I am in favor of the death penalty when it comes to people hitting my car.

Apparently I don't have an anger problem unless bad things happen to me.

**Day 153.** Insomnia is my nemesis, but I'm working on it. I've read books and *Reader's Digest* articles about it, and I lie awake thinking about them.

Last night I lay here for about an hour going over Psalm 23, thinking about each word. Then I counted sheep. Then I talked to the Shepherd. Nothing worked. I was sorely tempted to play Pac-Man, but instead I turned on the TV and found women's curling. Out like a light.

**Day 154.** Ramona's birthday is getting closer. I thanked the social networking friends for their suggestions and told them what I bought her:

- a thirty-dollar gift certificate to the Home Depot plumbing section
- an ironing board—the old one was real squeaky
- a ringtone of me speaking at a church
- a puzzle with a portrait of ME!
- a box of frozen waffles, so she doesn't have to cook— just pop them in the toaster!
- an alarm clock—she overslept twice last year
- a certificate for one free vacuuming, good for a year
  I will vacuum the car!

The women who commented on my list weren't so keen. There was an ominous warning from one: "Buy warm clothes and blankets; you'll be spending the night in the doghouse."

But the men loved it. One had another suggestion: "Nothing revives the dying embers like an inbuilt Vacuflo!"

A whole-house vacuum. That rings a bell.

**Day 155.** I had better success in the church parking lot today. I spotted two station wagons.

Once indoors, I appeared to be listening intently to the sermon, but how could I? Two rows forward sat the owner of a station wagon. He is a notoriously horrid driver. You connect the dots.

Should I confront him or just let the matter drop?

If I bring things to light, I will be vindicated and a problem will be solved that has unsettled me since I forgave the elderly complainant three weeks ago. I don't think I should allow the confusion to continue. I mean, what if my aged brother begins warning others of my bad driving—not as a matter of gossip, but in the interest of personal safety? "You need to stay away from Callaway in the parking lot," he might announce.

Already I have noticed some suspicious glances.

Where will this end? If I must confess all my uncharitable thoughts about people, thoughts I have not expressed or acted upon, will I have time for anything else? I wish the elderly churchgoer would just ram the offending station wagon. That way, things would be easier for me.

In church I flipped to my concordance at the back of the Bible and located "forgiveness." There was something about confessing our sins to one another, but nothing about offering vicarious forgiveness. Or confronting someone who may have reason to gossip, but probably hasn't done so.

I caught snippets of the sermon, something about leaving our cares with God, that God is big enough. I remained unconvinced, but thought I'd better give it a go.

Afterward, we drove slowly out of the parking lot. "What's come over you?" Ramona asked. "You hardly ever use your blinkers."

**Day 156.** I got carried away tonight. "I'm speaking in Florida in a few months," I told Paul, my son's smoking friend. "The family's coming with me, and I want you to join us. We'll sit under palm trees on sandy beaches while your friends back home huddle in their igloos." (Like us, Paul lives in western Canada.)

He almost popped two blood vessels in his forehead. "I've never been south of Sweet Grass, Montana," he said. "Or Bald Butte."

"There's one condition," I cautioned. "You have to quit."

"Smoking?"

"No. Playing Yahtzee. Yes, smoking."

"When?"

"Um…Wednesday."

"Whoa!" he said. "I'll go for a walk and think about it."

**Day 157.** I can't stop playing Pac-Man. I asked my son if he wanted to play. "Are you kidding?" he said. "That thing's addictive. I have enough problems in my life."

Wonder if there's an online support group.

I forced myself to shut down the computer and pulled out the vacuum. After operating the appliance in several rooms, I went to bed early.

"You sure seem cheery," I said to my wife.

"Come 'ere," she replied.

**Day 158.** There's a preacher on TV who was telling a massive audience that God wants us to prosper financially, never be sick, and have only good relationships. The preacher seemed like a nice guy. And I like money. And health. And friendship.

If God will do this for me, I will love him forever! Maybe God wants me to sell as many books as the TV preacher does. And drive the same model car he drives. Oh, I know that money won't buy happiness, but if I had enough of the stuff, I could hire a research staff to study the problem.

Dear God: Send me a sign that you want me RICH!

**Day 159.** This evening after a long walk, Paul took his last drag on a cigarette. "Good-bye forever," he said.

**Day 160.** Still no sign that God wants me rich. Nuts!

In lieu of the perfect birthday gift, I bought Ramona the most expensive bar of dark chocolate I could find and slapped a Post-it note on it that said, "You're sweeter than this. —PC. "

Then I hid it in her drawers drawer.

**Day 161.** Ramona's birthday all day today. I tried to keep her out of the kitchen, but she kept walking through offering suggestions. I burned the stupid brownies. Could use them for hockey pucks, I suppose. But all the kids were home, that's what she most wanted. I gave her a neck massage during the first half of the football game. And presented her with more dark chocolate. Then we watched *Marley and Me,* so she got to see me frighteningly close to tears.

Rachael gave Ramona a handmade card. It says, "I love you so much, Mom. Thank you for making this home a place I love to come back to. I hope I age as gracefully as you."

Wish I'd have thought of that. This really is a place I love to come home to. And as far as aging goes, Ramona is often mistaken for my daughter.

**Day 162.** On the flight home from a speaking engagement, I read John Piper's book *Don't Waste Your Life* and decided never to play Pac-Man ever again. I swear. Just to be certain, I took a self-administered Internet-addiction test and passed with flying colors:

- Do you stay online longer than you intended? Check.
- Do you neglect household chores to go online? Check.
- Do people in your life complain about the time you spend online? Check.
- Do you sometimes lose sleep because you are online? Check.
- Have you ever seen little blue dots when you close your eyes at night? Check.
- Do you snap, yell, or become annoyed if someone interrupts you while you're online? No. (But given a little more time, I could achieve this.)

Arriving home I served notice to the family that they can call me on the carpet if they catch me wasting time on Pac-Man even one more time.

The nightly news reported that a politician had been caught in an affair. My first response was, "What an idiot." My second response was, "What separates me from him? Grace? Opportunity?"

Good old C. S. Lewis had it right: "We are half-hearted creatures, fooling about with drink and sex and ambition when infinite joy is offered us, like an ignorant child who wants to go on making mud pies in the slum because he cannot imagine what is meant by the offer of a holiday at the sea. We are far too easily pleased."[1]

**Day 163.** Been reading the Bible as part of my rigorous Pac-Man–withdrawal program. I've paid careful attention, but so far have yet to encounter anything resembling what the TV preacher promised. If God wants us wealthy, why didn't Jesus have a house? If God wants us healthy, why did Paul have a thorn and Jesus get stripped and beaten, ridiculed and scorned? Why did the apostle John slave away in rock quarries on Patmos?

I read the story of a Chinese saint who was imprisoned and assigned to slosh around in the sewer. He gave thanks that he smelled so bad! That way, the guards stayed away from him and he could sing songs to God as loudly as he wanted.

Tonight my son Steve mentioned his friends in Africa who love Jesus and live in cardboard houses.

I still haven't given up hope, though. Maybe tomorrow God will give me that sign.

**Day 164.** Today Isaac Walker sat in my office telling me how much money he is making doing nothing. It's like he's found a loophole in mortality.

Is this a sign or what?

A few months back, he invested in a wonderful online company that sells trinkets on eBay, and he is becoming repulsively rich. How rich? He's only too happy to show me.

He signs in to a Web site that tallies his earnings by the day, flaunting what he has accrued while he drinks coffee, trims his toenails, or sleeps.

"Unbelievable," he groaned. I can see a grin reflected in the computer monitor. "I am earning 1 percent a day for doing absolutely nothing! It's a little risky, but hey…"

We talked about other stuff, of course, but now I can't think of anything else. Terms like "ground floor" and "compound interest" and "exotic vacation" are swirling through my mind. I am calculating how much I can scrape together for an investment, and how much pleasure I would derive from sitting around watching money pile up.

More bothersome than missing this opportunity is knowing that an adventuresome friend has seized it and is rolling around in the stuff. I once saw an ad for an investment book. It said, "Never again will a friend earn more than you."

Compare up, not down.

I'm no mathematician, but if I plunk down $10,000 I can triple it by next Christmas.

**Day 165.** Ramona said something intolerable tonight. She suggested that perhaps my former friend, the one who now specializes in betrayal, has been dealing with some tough stuff in his life, and just maybe he is lashing out on account of that. She says he needs God's grace and I'm not so perfect either.

I snorted and said something derisive. Am I self-centered, or is it just me?

**Day 166.** I talked to my wife about the iron-clad Internet-investment opportunity that Isaac is involved in.

"I think it's a gift of God," I found myself saying.

She shook her head. "Sounds like a scam to me. Why do they need money from you? Why don't they go to a bank?"

Ramona knows nothing about the intricacies of investing.

"Well, you know banks," I said, rolling my eyes.

"Did you pray about it?" she inquired.

I said a quick prayer and answered: "Yes."

"We can multiply the money like loaves and fishes, then pass it out to needy people." I wasn't lying. I have moments when I really think of doing this.

She shook her head again. "Sounds fishy."

"I'll give 15 percent of it to God."

This time she seemed genuinely impressed.

I could hardly sleep thinking about all the people we could help with all that cash. All those needy kids. Like my own.

**Day 167.** Ramona and I will leave soon for five days in Hong Kong (population 44 billion), where I am to speak at an educators' conference, a business breakfast, and a church. I wish I were more thankful for these opportunities. The truth is, I'm worn out. Also, I'm worried about Ramona's health. The last three seizures she's had were in the wake of the exhaustion brought on by international travel. Is it wrong to pray that God will bump us up to first class, where they will bring us the head of a pig, and on fine china too? Does God care about such things?

I'll pray lots and see.

My investor friend, Isaac, has assured me that I can still get in on the Golden Online Investment blessing when we return home. Next Christmas we could go anywhere first class. I wouldn't have to trouble God about it.

**Day 169.** Sunday, 12:16 p.m. Milton Russell is an old-timer at our church who loves to tell me corny jokes, like the one about the two peanuts that were assaulted.

For two years Milton has e-mailed me lame jokes, and almost every Sunday he pulls me aside after morning worship with a real knee-slapper. "I save my best ones for you," he grins, which is a bit like hearing you've won a vacuum cleaner demonstration.

Today Milton could barely get through his joke, he was so excited. "Did you hear about the short fortune-teller who escaped from prison?"

I hadn't.

"She was a small medium at large. Ha! Ha! Ha!"

I chuckled politely, but that's all I could manage. Milton looked disappointed, like he had thrown me his best pitch and I didn't swing. But when you've taken a truth vow, you can't laugh at something you don't find funny.

Actually, that was the least of my challenges today. The elderly gentleman who accused me of driving a station wagon and nearly colliding with him in the church parking lot was parked near us.

"New car?" he asked when he saw me.

I paused. "Yes." It's new to me.

"Have a good week," he said.

Did I detect a hint of sarcasm? I'm pretty sure he saw the dent in my side panel. He probably thinks I should have my license revoked.

11:53 p.m. I have spent a lot of time thinking about first class, praying about first class, claiming first class, speaking it into existence. Even checked the Internet for last-minute upgrades, in case God wasn't listening.

But as we were about to board, a flight attendant called me over and tore up our tickets. Before I had time to object, he handed me new ones. We clambered aboard to find we had been bumped not to first class, where you need binoculars to see other passengers, but to business class, where you can still seat a family of eight and a herd of cats.

Hot towels! Warm almonds! White slippers! A reclining massage chair for each of us! A flight attendant brought a small suitcase of toiletries and asked, "Is there anything else you need, Mr. Callaway?"

"Um...more almonds," was all I could think of.

I turned to Ramona in a recliner across the aisle and said way too loudly, "God loves us!"

Then I pelted her with almonds.

Peasant passengers trudging past us to the cattle car frowned at me. I smiled at them, knowing how they felt. If only they had more faith.

**Day 171.** With Christmas fast approaching, we've begun the annual quest for a list of necessities that advertisers are convincing us we'll be miserable without.

Sadly, I couldn't think of one solitary item I need, so I asked Ramona for lots of love and attention in the coming year—and some foot-rub coupons. She said she would settle for buying me a watch, because mine hasn't kept time since April.

Talk about good timing. Here in Hong Kong they sell watches by the shipload. Today in the Mongkok Market in Kowloon, I found a place where you can stand, swivel your head, and see nothing but shiny watches in all four directions. You also can see three million people packed into an area the size of a cricket pitch.

A stranger asked, "You want copy watch?"

I didn't know what that meant, but said, "Sure."

"We have three kinds. Fake. Fake fake. And genuine fake."

"I'm no cheapskate," I laughed. "I want genuine fake."

She pulled out a thick catalog.

Wow. Rolex! Tag Heuer! Gucci!

I asked for a Rolex. Total price? Twenty dollars. Savings? More than $90,000! What a deal! Ramona purchased two small Louis Vuitton purses for a pittance. In no time we saved another $5,000.

Back at our hotel, I looked over some notes for tomorrow's

meeting, where I'll speak on "Making Life Rich Without Money." Then I checked the watch. It was still ticking.

**Day 172.** Breakfast is served in a room atop a skyscraper in Hong Kong's famed banking district. Everyone loves my watch.

It has been a bad year for finance here in Hong Kong too. Who knows when the downward spiral will end? The room is encased in glass, overlooking the harbor. I said to Ben, my host: "If I were scouting for a movie set, I'd pick this."

"They already have," he said. "Used it in the Batman movie *The Dark Knight.*"

One financier leaned over to me when my speech was over. "I'm happier since I lost a few million," he whispered. "God has done amazing things when money got out of the way. I quit chasing what doesn't satisfy, and I got my wife back."

The evening was spent cruising Hong Kong Harbor and eating the head of an ox. Well, maybe not the head, but just about everything else. As we watched the light show, complete with a thirty-story blinking Santa Claus, I talked with two sisters who grew up in China. They were unable to speak aloud about political matters—even in their own house—for fear of being hauled off to jail. "The police used to give us three choices," one said. "Jail, beating, or a fine of fifteen dollars."

"Let me guess what you chose."

They laughed. "We watched them count the money, then cross the street and enter a restaurant, smiling. Of course, it didn't always work out that well."

Others confided that they had been beaten and imprisoned because they follow Jesus. They were telling me their stories not from pride or want of attention. "We are so thankful to have suffered for him," they said.

As I flipped off the light in our hotel room, I thought: *Today I was with people whose feet I am unworthy to wash.*

I checked the watch. Still ticking.

**Day 173.** 1:30 p.m. I had to show off my great purchase to new friends Janet and Ruth. "What's really amazing," I told them, "is that many of these copy watches will work fine for years. I have a friend who spent five dollars on a New York Gucci in 1979 and it's still ticking." Just then I experienced a wristband malfunction. The Rolex disintegrated and hit the floor like a misfiring James Bond cuff link.

Janet and Ruth hadn't seen anything this hilarious in their entire lives. They laughed for a solid minute, holding their stomachs, gasping for air. Apparently, the humor here is different.

"I guess I'll have to take it back," I suggested while gathering pieces off the floor.

This just set them off again.

"Mongkok Market has a twenty-four-hour guarantee," said Janet.

"Let's go," I said. "We can still make it."

2:30 p.m. Somehow I found the same Copy Watch Lady in the market. She seemed completely puzzled that my watch had fallen apart. This has never happened before! She offered me a new one. "Fo you? No poblem! No chauj!"

I bought two more watches, one for each of the boys. My Christmas shopping was done.

Ramona picked up another Louis Vuitton for Rachael. We spent another forty-four dollars and saved nearly $200,000!

8:30 p.m. Wesley M e-mailed to say that his Internet-dating thing is showing some promise. He mentioned in his profile that he is a man of faith, and the service linked him up with a girl of like faith. I told him I'd keep my fingers crossed.

"Pray too," he chided.

"Oh yes, that's what I meant." Which was a lie. So I apologized for lying. Then I prayed that this girl would be the mate of Wesley's dreams.

9:30 p.m. We watched a few minutes of a documentary on torture. It was in Chinese with Mandarin subtitles.

I thought about my former friend who is still spreading rumors about me, and my anger grew. I prayed that God would send salamanders to infest his bathtub, and load his mailbox with lots of letters. From the tax people.

"Lord, give him jury duty."

Is this wrong? I'm quite certain it is. But stopping is hard.

10:30 p.m. I checked all three watches. Still ticking!

**Day 174.** I've been so excited about the great time we're having in Hong Kong that I forget to pray for a bump to business class on the way home. I hoped that God would hear my unspoken request, but apparently not. Seated in row 463, Ramona mentioned how cool it is that no matter where we go, we find people who love Jesus and now there are a bunch of them scattered all over the bottom half of the world. "Everywhere we go," she said, "I pray we'll be a blessing. And end up getting blessed."

Sometimes, in those rare moments of honesty, I admit that my prayer is different. I pray that everywhere we go, we'll sell lots of books.

Then I had to shake the doggone watch to make it start ticking again.

**Day 176.** Sunday, 8 a.m. I tried to get out of bed for church. Couldn't move my fingers or eyelids. Was pretty sure I'd had a stroke.

1 p.m. More positive than ever that I'd had a stroke, but couldn't move to tell my wife and couldn't pick up the phone to call anyone.

3 p.m. Had healed enough to stagger to the kitchen, eat two pieces of raw bread and a hunk of cheese, then staggered back. The phone rang. Who cares?

10:30 p.m. Wide awake. Ready to roll. I made a few calls. Then apologized. Someone asked why I hadn't been at church. "Slept in," I said. "I may have had a stroke."

## Honest Confession #6

I have liked money all my life. Oh sure, I know that it won't make me rich, make me happy, buy me love, or buy what it used to. I have taught that it makes a lousy servant but a great master, and I agree wholeheartedly with myself. But still I like it. I have some in the bank, and it's nice to know it's there, just in case. I think the times I've trusted God the best are when I've had to trust him the most. And we haven't had to in a while. Not in the financial department.

This year I've been looking at the multitude of Bible verses about lying and the tongue. In many cases money is not far off. Agur ben Jakeh compiled some sayings in Proverbs. Here are a few I like:

O God, I beg two favors from you;
    let me have them before I die.
First, help me never to tell a lie.
    Second, give me neither poverty nor riches!
    Give me just enough to satisfy my needs.
For if I grow rich, I may deny you and say,
        "Who is the LORD?"
    And if I am too poor, I may steal and thus
        insult God's holy name.[2]

I've prayed this prayer many times. Still I like money. Just being honest.

# SEVEN

# Angels for Christmas

Pretty much all the honest truth telling in the world is done by children.

—OLIVER WENDELL HOLMES

The truth brings with it a great measure of absolution, always.

—R. D. LAING

**Day 177.** I was still suffering a jet-lag hangover but somehow managed to answer the phone. Mom was yelling over the phone line: "Are you coming for Halloween?"

Halloween was more than a month ago.

I told her I'd be picking her up for Christmas Eve.

"Fine," she said, then the dementia really kicked in: "Don't forget to bring the ice from the curtain plunger."

**Day 178.** Four hundred thirty-one e-mails. One from a missionary friend reminding me that we can spend money on ourselves this Christmas or, for the price of a Mongkok watch, help ten street kids in the Philippines have a party complete with games, gifts, and a goose. I mentioned to Ramona that this is just guilt-mongering, but then softened and said maybe we should pray about it.

She said, "Why would you pray about something God says we should do?"

While I chastened her for speaking in that tone of voice, she wrote out a check. I watched her. One hundred dollars! Unbelievable. But she wasn't finished. Another zero. One thousand doggone dollars! All our book sales from Hong Kong!

While climbing into bed, I stepped on little shards of metal. My Rolex. It was in thirty-four pieces on the floor.

**Day 179.** Since Paul quit smoking, he is experiencing two warring emotions. First, he feels like he is going to die. Second, his lungs hurt so bad, he is afraid he won't.

He wants to lunge from tall buildings. He wants to smoke anything he can get in his mouth. Everything he sees reminds him of cigarettes. French fries. Cucumbers. Egg cartons. But tonight he admits, "I feel great. I'm happier. I'm nicer to be around."

And he is. The boy is a different man.

Thank you, God! If you can change Paul, there's hope for me!

**Day 180.** Our church's resident eschatological wizard, Ernest Winkler, phoned to tell me that one of the winning Illinois lottery numbers was 666. Barack Obama is from Illinois. Hmm.

**Day 181.** I found my mother, lonesome and wondering who I am. Lately she's been totally coherent, except when she's awake. When I visit, she won't speak to me at first. Instead, she informs the lamp: "He left his wife, you know. He's been stealing from me. Yes, he's a thief."

Most of our conversation is surreal, like I am in some parallel universe on the Space channel where I need a language decoder. "Yes, he's taken everything, even washing the floors and bunions."

Then she turns to me and says, "Daddy, it's good to see you!"

**Day 182.** A week after visiting Hong Kong, I am speaking at the annual Chinese Business Association's Christmas Banquet. The opening is a complete disaster. "My mother started walking a mile a day when she was seventy-three," I said. "She's eighty-five now, and we don't know where she is."

Nary a snicker.

"We have three children. One of each."

Not a sound.

"Had our three children in three years. We're far more satisfied than the guy with $3 million. How so? The guy with $3 million wants more."

I'm going over like an attack of the hiccups in church.

Members of the audience smile politely and dart their eyes at one another. Two minutes in, I fully expect to be pinned to the wall with stainless steel utensils, so, in an act of desperation, I discard my notes, clear my throat, and say, "Ramona and I are just back from Hong Kong. We loved it there. Has anyone been to Hong Kong?"

The place comes to life. It is the funniest thing I have said in my life.

"Has anyone been to the Mongkok Market?"

This is funnier still. The place explodes. They laugh so hard they need oxygen. They have to loosen their ties.

"I bought a watch there... Look!" I hold up my arm and fear the building might collapse from the audience outburst. I've never heard anything like it.

To this day, if you ask members of the Chinese Business Association who is the funniest man on earth, there's no doubt they will point to me. "Ha, ha! He bought Rolex! Ha, ha! In Mongkok Market! I need my heart pills!"

Afterward, a dear elderly lady leaned on her cane and asked me, "Did you find your mother yet?"

**Day 183.** Fellow worshipers are extraordinarily glad to see me. A few said they heard I had a stroke. Two of them said they've been praying for me. Well, yeah. I was rendered nearly immobile by jet lag, but I hadn't literally had a stroke.

What does God do with those prayers?

I filled out a visitor's card to place in the offering plate. Under the section "What can we do for you?" I wrote, "I am not a visitor, but I would certainly like some pie. That would help me be even more happy here in this church."

I signed it with my rightful name, gave my address and phone number, then added, "the best time to bring it is anytime before 6 p.m."

**Day 184.** With Christmas fast approaching, I know I'll need money, so the Golden Internet-Investment opportunity has been heavy on my mind. Today I threw all kinds of fleeces before God, opportunities for him to stop me from investing in the Internet windfall if it isn't his will.

"Lord, if our home-Internet connection crashes and stays down for twenty-four hours, I will be unable to register and will not invest.

"If the bank will not certify my check, that will be a sign.

"If Isaac calls today saying he's lost all his money, I shall withhold funds."

**Day 185.** All the fleeces are dry, so I sent in a check for a sizeable sum. As I dropped it in the mail, I prayed, "Lord, multiply this, and I'll invest in your kingdom. I really will. I will help others. I will give...um...20 percent. I'd like to take some trips to Hawaii, but you can have the rest. Amen."

I claimed the blessing, then rebuked the enemy of unbelief.

**Day 186.** Since I bought those stupid Rolex watches in Hong Kong, every one has conked out. I started to wind one today and the pin popped out. At least it isn't a grenade.

Ramona put my low-cost Wal-Mart wristwatch through the wash—an accident, I think. It's still ticking, but the numbers are gone and the face turned clockwise about half an hour.

I remember that back in July I promised myself I'd make this the very best Christmas in the history of Christmases. Wish I could remember how I was going to make it happen.

Can't think of a thing I want for Christmas except sitting down for twenty minutes without someone phoning, beeping, texting, tweeting, e-mailing, or Facebooking me. I'd also like a watch that isn't fast, though I have been on time for an unusually high volume of appointments.

**Day 187.** I'm trying to visit Mom at least once a week. Usually I manage it. The worst part of visiting is leaving. It's okay when someone's with me, because Mom seems to pull up her socks and put on a good front. But when I'm alone and I say good night, tears cloud her eyes and she reaches out and says, "Don't go."

So I sit and read to her from her large-print Bible, carefully editing the psalms, sticking with those that remind us of God's enduring faithfulness and mercy and avoiding the imprecatory ones where David declares, "Happy shall he be, that taketh and dasheth thy little ones against the stones,"[1] something you don't read to pregnant women like my eight-five-year-old mother.

I uttered a bedtime prayer tonight before I left. It was the same blessing she blessed me with a thousand times:

> The LORD bless thee, and keep thee:
> The LORD make his face shine upon thee, and be gracious unto
>     thee:
> The LORD lift up his countenance upon thee, and give thee peace.[2]
> Amen.

I tried to replace the "thees" with "yous," but she would have none of it, registering her displeasure by reaching out and pinching my cheek. Hard. When I said good night, she looked disappointed, not that I was leaving but that I would attempt to improve upon the old King James.

"Good night, Mom. Sleep tight. Don't let the bedbugs bite."

She smiled when I said that and blew kisses as I backed out the door, wondering how long it will be until that's me lying there, my forehead scrunched because my son keeps leaving out the best part of the book of Psalms, the brutally honest parts.

**Day 188.** At 5:15 p.m. our doorbell rang. It was the church secretary carrying an apple pie.

"I can't believe you did this! You really shouldn't have!"

But she insisted and handed it to me, saying, "It is more blessed to give than to receive."

I said, "Yes, but sometimes it is very blessed to receive."

I love this church. I am going to take better notes during sermons and stop whining about the music.

**Day 189.** Great news today: Wesley M's Internet dating is going well. This girl is everything a guy could hope for. They share so much in common, you couldn't write a script that's any better. He is cautiously ecstatic. I'm so happy for him. Maybe matchmaking could be a new ministry for me.

**Day 190.** At church Milton Russell grabbed me by the shoulder and towed me over to the coatrack for our postservice joke time. I could hardly wait.

"Did you hear about the cannibal that ate the missionary?"

I hadn't.

"He got a taste of religion."

I patted Milton's shoulder and smiled like a televangelist. I think he thinks I think this was the funniest thing I'd heard in a while, something that is so funny I can't catch my breath to laugh out loud. He seemed encouraged and said, "I'll do even better next week. See if I can find a seasonal joke."

The suspense may kill me.

**Day 191.** The annual Christmas brag letter finally arrived from the Thompsons (not their real name; their real name is the

Fergusons). I've dreaded opening this envelope since last Christmas. The letter lists their kids' GPAs, sports honors won, mission trips taken, and number of souls saved. Their four kids are so smart they will most likely run the world in just a few years. The eldest is in medical school, then there is an assortment of potential dentists and teachers, plus the youngest who will likely hold the keys to nuclear warfare.

No family makes me feel more like a failure.

Maybe my expectations are too low. Until this letter arrived, I was celebrating another year of our children staying out of jail.

**Day 192.** On the fourth day of Christmas, my true love said to me, "Let's change Christmas up a bit by having just one gift each this year. Keep it simple. Have some lonely people in for Christmas dinner. There are lots of them at church." I love my wife and appreciate her compassion.

I smiled like I completely agreed. Technically, the smile was not a lie. Though it could be argued that a lie consists of deception, which does not require words.

**Day 193.** I booted up the computer to check on something legitimate, but on the right side of the screen there was an ad for Pac-Man. I've been doing so well. Was this merely a coincidence or could it be a test? I settled on it being providence and decided to play to 50,000 points. I chomped and gnawed and munched, and soon an hour had been swallowed into eternity. It was embarrassing.

I heard Ramona approaching, so I quickly pushed Pause and changed screens to an Oswald Chambers devotional, but Ramona knew something was amiss and leaned over my shoulder to look at the minimized windows indicators along the bottom of the screen.

"Aha!" she said, before leaving the room. That's all. Amazing how much guilt one word can summon.

**Day 194.** Today I listened to a talk-radio program while I was driving. Two believers were arguing about whether to boycott Christmas. I wanted to call in, but was unsure of what to say and didn't have a phone with me. Did Jesus boycott certain businesses on account of their advertising campaigns? We don't know. Was he loved by business owners? I think so. Except for the money-changers. Did the disciples display a fish symbol on the stern of their boats?

Ernest Winkler, the end-times expert at church, is the guy who told me to listen to this radio show. Ernest insists that the world is going to hell so fast that we had better huddle together in colonies of like-minded people, eat prunes, boycott the bad guys, and read books about the end times while hoping that Jesus returns before any of the big persecutions get started. (When I was twenty-one and about to be married, my greatest fear was that Jesus would return and take us to heaven before my wedding night.)

Did Jesus say, "Cower," or did he say, "Go"? Maybe one day I'll summon the nerve to ask Ernest about it.

**Day 195.** My wife insisted on pasting the Fergusons' family portrait to our fridge. They've doctored the thing, you can tell. No one in the real world has teeth that straight and white. They beam at me every time I make myself a snack plate, reminding me of all I will never have or be, reminding me that my teeth still hurt from trying to bleach them for the class reunion.

**Day 196.** I don't know about you, but I get whiney sometimes. This morning I was feeling sorry that I won't have my dad around this Christmas. I griped to Ramona about it as we walked to our town's exercise facility. (Normally we drive… Is that called irony?) She already bought a big turkey out of habit, and we invited a few people to join us for Christmas. But the invitations came back, stamped undeliverable. (How can so many people move every year?) Ramona said we should pray that God would show us whom to invite, but I'm thinking, *God has enough to do. I won't trouble him.*

We went to a sandwich shop for lunch to replenish the calories we burned off on the elliptical. Sitting alone, off to the side, was an eightyish man I hadn't seen before. But he recognized me as a writer. We exchanged pleasantries.

"Merry Christmas," I said.

"It will be a tough one." He looked down at the table. "My wife is battling Alzheimer's in a hospital up north. I had to take her there two years ago yesterday. I visit when I can—"

God lifted my hat and flicked me on the ear.

"Do you have any family around?" I asked.

"Nope."

I wrote my name and phone number on a piece of paper with the words *Christmas Dinner* underlined.

"We'd love to have you at our place," I told the stranger. His eyes were already misty, and now tears started trickling down his cheeks.

"Please phone me," I told him. "I don't wanna have to go looking for you." From time to time I find myself doing the right thing and wonder what has come over me.

I called my daughter and told her about it. "Thanks, Daddy," she said. "I could really use a grandpa right now. Can't wait to meet him!"

I told a friend about all this, and he got so excited he brought over a turkey. I didn't have the heart to tell him we already have one.

**Day 197.** I love the songs of Christmas. This morning the church's teenage worship band was playing them at 300 decibels, but no one seemed to mind. Evidently, "The Little Drummer Boy" had a full set with Zylgian cymbals and some amplification.

Milton was nowhere to be found afterward, so I heard no bad jokes. Phew.

Despite Pastor Rod's exhortation to reach out to the needy, I told Ramona that I was real tired this year, maybe burning out. I mentioned that I'd really like a Christmas where we keep the visitors to a minimum, where we pray for people whose photos are on our fridge, but leave it at that.

"Would that be too much to ask?" I concluded. "Mom will be

here Christmas Eve and she's a handful. Who knows what she'll accuse me of?"

**Day 198.** 2:10 p.m. I composed an e-mail for Mr. Ferguson of the Perfect Christmas Letter Fergusons: "Why don't you send out a Christmas letter that humans can identify with? God had a rough go with his first kids, you know?"

Then I remembered my father's advice about leaving negative letters in a drawer for three days before mailing them. So I pushed Delete and opted for this instead: "Congratulations on your year. Mine sucked. Investments through the floorboards. Mom's in sad shape. I've been wondering if my kids will amount to anything. Marriage good, but sometimes we fight like Itchy and Scratchy. Is there hope for us?"

On the holiday front, still no word from our adopted grandpa. A friend says he thinks the old guy was an angel, that he was sent to test us.

Hmm. For once, I may have passed.

3:05 p.m. Received an e-mail from Mr. Ferguson. He wrote: "Our year wasn't so hot either. Faye and I are likely going to separate, and our son just moved in with a girl who has some cats and tattoos and won't speak to us. I've envied your family for years. Would you please pray for ours?"

A horrible thought crossed my mind as I stood in front of the fridge, staring at the Fergusons' perfect family portrait. I hate to admit it, but the horrible thought was this: *Ha!*

Then I spent considerable time repenting and offered up a prayer for the Fergusons.

There was still no word from Angel Grandpa. Maybe my friend is right. But wouldn't that be something? I would be credited for a genuine act of kindness and could still spend a quiet Christmas humming "Silent Night."

I repented for this thought too.

**Day 199.** I took my family to the mall to experience the joy of frenzied shopping. Aisle 11 had a guy selling knives. If you buy one, you get four. Pretty good deal. My wife could use a knife. I bought two and got eight. Who will I give them to? My mother? The salesman leaned toward my daughter, Rachael, and said: "Finish school or you'll end up selling knives in a mall."

The girl beeping our purchases through the checkout said, "Did you find everything you were looking for?"

Truth serum kicked in and I said, "No. I didn't find peace, joy, and happiness here. Do you have those?"

She raised one eyebrow, then laughed.

Rachael suddenly took undue interest in a copy of *National Enquirer* and pretended to be the daughter of the man behind me, who bought four knives and got sixteen.

Finally! A call from our new grandfather! He confirmed that he would join us for Christmas dinner and added that he would come by later to drop off a turkey. I didn't have the heart to tell him we already have two. I wonder if he needs any knives.

**Day 200.** Christmas Eve!

Decided to conduct an informal survey while finishing some last-minute shopping. When clerks greeted me with "Happy holidays!" I mustered my kindest smile and said a cheery "Merry Christmas." Eleven of thirteen store clerks returned the favor. It caused me to feel so joyful that I decided not to boycott anyone.

We had the Christmas Eve party at our house. Mom can't sign her name to checks any longer, but I can. I have power of attorney. She gave each of her grandkids a nice bonus this year. They lined up and thanked her with a kiss. Mom told me years ago that she just barely wanted to outlive her money, so I'm doing my part.

**Day 201.** The kids are at the age where it's tough to wake them, even on Christmas morning. This time, I got a little worried when I tried to wake my son Steve. Thought at first he was in a coma. When he was a kid, he started waking me up about 4 a.m., asking if he could open gifts. That was in October. Those days are gone.

I conducted the traditional protracted prelude to presents, which has served to drive my offspring nuts through the years: Eat breakfast. Clean off table. Wipe dishes. Sweep floor. Vacuum. Wash walls. Gather to read gospel of Luke. Memorize gospel of Luke. In Portuguese. And finally, the avalanche of gifts.

By noon there are so many people here we need nametags. I bet some of them just wandered in because my son left the door open and they smelled turkey.

I unwrapped a watch. Family members had pooled their resources. "You'll never have to buy another," the salesman had told my wife. "It is solar-paneled and eco-friendly. No trees were killed in the making of this timepiece; you'll never need to change the oil."

The new grandpa arrived in time to watch me trim the bird. He didn't seem to notice it wasn't his turkey. Christmas dinner this year was a laying-on of goodness.

Jeff departed with his girlfriend. He left the door open, and it was four hundred below zero, He can't think straight when she's around.

I yelled, "Hey, were you born in a barn?"

He hollered back, "Jesus was. Merry Christmas, Dad!"

All in all, a pretty good day.

Note to self: Christmas isn't my birthday.

**Day 203.** It has taken about two weeks, but my ridiculously lucrative Internet Golden Investment account is up and running. I can go online 24/7 and check to see just how much money is being funneled into my pockets. Today—a Saturday—I earned 1 percent! Sounds paltry, but it compounds daily. I came up with a tidy little spreadsheet so I can forecast my investment future. Unbelievable.

I feel so guilty I almost need to see a priest.

How much was I going to give to God? Ten percent, I think it was.

The one cloud in the sky is some bad news from Wesley M regarding his Internet-dating partner. The girl of his dreams turned out to be his cousin.

I tried to console him over the phone, but the humor of the situation began to tug at my funny bone, and I had to stifle a laugh. This may just be the funniest coincidence I have witnessed. Ever.

**Day 204.** I was sick today, so church was out of the question. It's the turkey, I bet. Maybe we should have used our new grandpa's bird. Or was my friend trying to poison me by way of his donated turkey? And will concerned church members assume that, with me absent, I've had another stroke? Will they pray?

Somehow, I summoned enough energy to watch some football.

**Day 205.** Today Paul couldn't look me in the eye. I sat him down and told him I'm not dumb. I'm old, but my nose still works.

"You've been smoking, haven't you?"

Sure enough, while he watched an Alfred Hitchcock movie where everyone smoked—including the train and small animals—Paul suffered a relapse.

"I'll give you one more chance," I told him.

"You shouldn't," he cautioned.

I reminded him of God's grace, how it comes to undeserving, bumbling people like me, and like him.

"So I can go to Florida with your family?"

"You betcha."

"I'll quit," he said, looking me straight in the eye.

"When?" I asked.

"Tomorrow. But right now I better go for a long walk."

**Day 206.** This daily checking on my growing pile of cash has become a borderline obsession. Years ago I wrote a book on how to be rich without money, for Pete's sake. But that was easy. I didn't have money then.

I wrote in that book, "Perhaps God is merciful enough to not bless us with it until he knows he can trust us with it."

So today I prayed that God would trust me and agreed to give 20 percent of all Internet Golden Investment earnings to his work.

**Day 207.** Today, New Year's Eve, Paul Turner took his last, last puff. Praise the Lord!

I decided to read the Bible through this next year, and also promised myself I'll get a little more exercise.

There are moments when my old self keeps popping up. A late night card game with my children has me cheating. Cheating! But only when I'm losing. Or shuffling. Or when the game is in play.

The kids are shaking their heads. And laughing. So am I.

"What about that truth vow?" says the youngest.

Tomorrow a new year dawns. With hope for people like me.

## Honest Confession #7

Forty years I've been trying to live my faith, and though I'm thankful to report growth, I was hoping it would be easier. I'm like Paul the smoker and Paul the apostle. The things I know to do, I don't; the things I know not to do, I do.[3] Lord, help me.

I'm not sure how eager I would have been to sign on for a year of telling the truth if I had known how hard it would be to live without hypocrisy, turn the other cheek, walk the extra mile, give up my coat, do good to those who tick me off, and pick up my cross and follow Christ. Thankfully, we're not asked to do all these things under our own steam. God, by his Spirit, will help us. I need him more than ever.

# EIGHT

# Chasing Money, Chasing Grace

I have more money than my grandchildren's
grandchildren can spend.

—GARTH BROOKS

Grace defies reason and logic. Love interrupts,
if you like, the consequences of your actions,
which in my case is very good news indeed
because I've done a lot of stupid stuff.

—BONO

**D**ay 208. New Year's Day. Back in the old days, when men were men and women were tired of it, we never talked about exercise, we just did it. We ran and kicked and threw and swung and chopped and whacked whatever we could find (sometimes each other), then fell into bed at night, exhausted. Not anymore. No one calls me to play on their basketball team these days on account of petty grievances, such as the fact that I have no natural talent left and need to carry an oxygen tank even during free throws.

Tonight, Ramona and I went for a postfeast-and-fireworks walk, and I said, "What's missing?"

"Um, hot chocolate? I don't know."

"Kids."

"You want more kids?"

"No, listen. There are no children out here anymore. Remember when we were small and they had to herd us indoors on New Year's with threats and rifles? Nowadays, the kids are inside playing computer games and watching the idiot box."

I had to stop talking because I ran out of breath.

"You're winded," Ramona pointed out.

"I'll start exercising tomorrow," I wheezed.

"Here, hold on to my arm. Let's make a complete lap of the house again."

Reading my Bible doesn't wind me, so I read for twenty-five minutes and got a solid jump-start on the year.

**Day 209.** Rachael's man friend, Jordan, came by and fit in well but had a bad case of nerves. It was most noticeable when he was leaning against the counter and the toast popped up. You'd have thought the boy had licked an electric fence.

**Day 211.** Great worship service today. Someone sang, "It's all yours, God, yours, God, everything,,,"[1] Which made me think of the money I'm earning while sitting in church trying to guess what joke Milton has prepared for me.

Should I check the account later today? It's Sunday. But eBay doesn't take a Sabbath, and it's the Lord's money anyway. It can't hurt.

The sermon was from Daniel. A miraculous story about three Hebrew guys who refused to worship an image of gold that the pagan king had set up. So they were thrown into a blazing furnace for their disobedience.

I breathed a sigh of relief that the sermon and the Old Testament saints' act of obedience to God were unrelated to money.

After the service, Milton was almost hyperventilating. He told me about the dog that gave birth to puppies downtown. Then he leaned in for the kill. "It was cited for littering!" His eyes widened expectantly.

By now I am so into the honesty thing that a bad joke doesn't draw a response from me. The laugh wouldn't come. Milton looked at me like you look at a little old lady accused of arson.

"Milton, I have taken a truth vow. How can I be completely truthful and laugh at a joke I do not find remotely funny?"

"My jokes aren't funny, they're punny." He smiled.

I started to laugh politely, then snapped out of it. "That's the last time. I will never laugh at one of your jokes again, unless you do better."

"Okay," he said. "I'm up to the challenge. You just wait."

**Day 212.** Had devotions again. Really, it shouldn't be a problem to read the Bible from start to finish this year. Our pastor says you can read it through in a year at about ten minutes a day.

**Day 213.** More devotions. I can do this.

**Day 214.** An author friend phoned with news about the latest review of her book and told me how it's scrambling up the bestseller list. I said, "Congratulations, that's wonderful!" But I was thinking, *Hey, you passed my book on your way to the top. Maybe I should travel from bookstore to bookstore, scouring shelves, hiding your book behind mine.*

I wouldn't say or do this, of course, but I did have a dream once where my book had hit number one, but another author's name was on the cover.

"Lord, help me improve my party skills."

I'm barely a week into the new year and already I'm aware of how badly I'll need grace. Someone once asked the evangelist D. L. Moody if he was filled with the Holy Spirit. He replied, "Yes, but I leak."

Me too.

**Day 215.** At the nursing home tonight, Mom was stuck on calling me a thief. I can't blame her. When I was nine or so, she asked me to run down to the newspaper office and buy several copies of that week's paper in which she had an article. She handed me two bucks—roughly a million dollars back then. Steve Porr accompanied me on the errand. As we passed the Dairy King, we could smell the aroma of candy wafting out the open windows. This presented a dilemma because God had so clearly provided us noses with which to appreciate the wafting, plus all this money from my mom.

As we stood by the road filling our faces with red-hot jawbreakers, Steve wanted to know my next move. "You just watch," I said. And he did. He watched me lie to my mother. I had the audacity to tell her that one of the big pagan kids in our town, a guy who smoked and drank, had threatened to beat us up if we didn't hand over all our money. It was going well for me, except every time I opened my mouth, she could see my teeth were stained red.

I was duly punished, but years later the dementia has summoned the memories back. Tonight she thinks I'm nine again and stealing her money.

"I'm sorry, Mom," I say. "I won't do it again." Which is a lie of sorts, I suppose.

She punches me hard on the arm and says, "Okay. You're a good boy. You can weed the garden now."

It's nice to be forgiven again for a decades-old crime, but my arm still hurts.

**Day 216.** I found out today that my former friend got tired of spreading rumors about me and instead tried to have me fired from my job. My boss laughed about it; I didn't.

I opened the Bible and found Psalm 35. It's perfect for my evening prayer time. I like it best in The Message:

Harass these hecklers, GOD,
　　punch these bullies in the nose.
Grab a weapon, anything at hand;
　　stand up for me!...

When those thugs try to knife me in the back,
　　make them look foolish....
Make their road lightless and mud-slick,
　　with GOD's angel on their tails....
Surprise them with your ambush—
　　catch them in the very trap they set,
　　the disaster they planned for me.

But let me run loose and free,
　　celebrating GOD's great work,
Every bone in my body laughing, singing, "God,
　　there's no one like you."[2]

Well said, David! Amen to that! Sing it again! Selah!

**Day 217.** This amassing of cash is like robbing a bank. Successful bank robbers are often discovered because they can't keep such great news to themselves, and I'm beginning to understand their dilemma.

A thought hits me: *If only I were this excited about Jesus! Wanting to tell everybody about him.* "Hey, look! He loves you! Invest in heaven and your investments won't rust or crack or fade or need Botox! It's right here in the Bible. You can check it every day."

Wonder who I could tell about the earthly investment. It's like the gospel. It's good news. Why would I keep it to myself?

**Day 218.** Milton was missing from church again. I hope he's okay. You don't suppose he could have died laughing at one of his own jokes? Or perhaps he's upset with my blunt honesty.

Sensing my disappointment over Milton's absence, my son Steve told me a joke that perfectly illustrates the dangers of complete honesty: Marge and Lester ended up single in the nursing home, though they had secretly loved each other since fifth grade. They probably would have gotten married, but blunt honesty did them in back in high school. Lester has a wooden eye, and when he asked Marge if she would like to accompany him to the prom, she exclaimed, "Would I! Would I!"

They never spoke again.

I tell it to a few people. Jokes are no good when you have to explain them. I wonder if Milton would get it.

**Day 219.** My old buddy Regi joined me in our town's aquatic center hot tub, and I couldn't help myself. I just had to tell him.

"You're earning how much doing *what?*" he asked, splashing me hard.

Regi is an agnostic when it comes to great investment opportunities. But he hadn't completely shut the door on belief; he was listening through the crack.

"Ya, I'm not kidding. You should see the guys who are into this. Good guys. Smart guys. Rich guys." There is water up my nose.

"But I thought you said *you* were in it?"

I tried to ignore this.

Later Regi called me from his house. He had gone online and was making noises normally associated with hyperventilation. He's almost in.

"I'm really wanting to help others with this," I said. "Maybe set up a foundation." I was being honest. I'd love to.

"I'm in," he said. "Thanks for telling me."

**Day 220.** Ramona wanted me to walk the dog, which was wearing a blue plaid sweater. There's no way I'll be caught dead walking a dog dressed in a sweater. My friends catch me and I will be beaten up as a matter of principle. So I told Ramona, "I will walk a dog in a sweater just as soon as I dress in a pink pantsuit and go to a quilting bee."

"I'd like to see that."

"Not a chance."

"But no one will see you. It's pitch black out."

"I will see me."

**Day 221.** A letter arrived from a ministry we support. In it was a little card my wife wedged into the bathroom mirror and pointed at while she flossed. It says:

Don't wear yourself out trying to get rich;
    restrain yourself!
Riches disappear in the blink of an eye;
    wealth sprouts wings
    and flies off into the wild blue yonder.

I flip it over and wedge it back in place. The other side says:

A faithful man
    will abound with blessings
But he who hastens to be rich
    will not go unpunished.[3]

"Let's give 15 percent," I said.

"You said you were gonna give 20 percent not long ago," she reminded me. Her memory's not so good.

**Day 222.** The good news: Regi has invested some money. The bad news: he's invested *more than I have*!

Haven't read the Bible for five days and am falling behind. At this rate I should get through Genesis this year.

**Day 223.** Spent the day delayed at fine airports everywhere because some idiot terrorist had explosives in his underpants. That never stopped Ramona and me from traveling when our kids were small. My sons often had explosives in their underpants.

**Day 225.** Milton grinned at me twice during the morning service, winked once during prayer, and waggled his head toward the foyer.

Before I could leave the sanctuary, he had me by the shirt and couldn't talk fast enough.

"O'Toole was driving down the street in a sweat because he had an important meeting and couldn't find a parking place."

"It's okay. Go slow," I coached. "Enunciate."

"O'Toole looks up to heaven and says, 'Lord, take pity on me. If you find me a parking place, I will go to Mass every Sunday for the rest of me life and give up me Irish whiskey!'

"Miraculously, a parking place appears. O'Toole looks up again and says, 'Never mind, Lord, I found me one.'"

I step back, away from the grip of Milton's hand, lift my head, and let go with a good honest cackle.

**Day 226.** A four-page letter arrived in response to a book I wrote called *Laughing Matters*. Here's a paragraph:

> Where do you read about the apostles trying to make jokes in order to reach people? Do you think they were hated by the world because they MADE PEOPLE LAUGH? The Bible contains no humor, why should you use it? I believe that many methods tried today are not according to the Bible and what the prophets of old and the apostles used. Jesus did use parables, but He certainly never MADE A JOKE about what was going on!
> Sincerely,
> Shandra

Actually, I'm not being completely honest. I changed her name. Her real name is Arlene. And maybe she's right. I wonder if Arlene is hated by the world. And I wonder if that is my mission on earth. What about "let your light so shine before men, that they may see your good works and glorify your Father in heaven"?[4] Will the world know we are his disciples because we are irritating, or because of our love?

**Day 227.** My family spent the day winging our way to Orlando, Florida. Former smoker Paul finally has a chance to hug a palm tree, swim in the Atlantic, and roast his white Canadian skin.

Paul has been telling complete strangers his story. In restaurants, in airplanes, in airports. He tells them that he feels better, that he's saving money, that God's grace is amazing, that they should check it out.

I told him he's such a great kid, we just might adopt him.

An American Airlines pilot left the cockpit because of "mental fatigue" and we were delayed four hours while a replacement arrived from California. Thankfully, the first pilot left the cockpit while we were on the ground.

Paul fidgeted a lot while we waited. Especially when he saw a pencil or a pen or anything cigarette shaped. In Dallas he almost lost his mind when someone stripped the plastic wrapping from a snack box.

**Day 228.** I'm still troubled about whether Arlene was right. Does the Bible contain humor? Maybe not. I e-mailed my doctoral candidate friend, James, about it, and he said the answer is a resounding yes. But there is a vast difference between the culture of the Bible and our culture. "The humor of the Bible usually has to do with wry Jewish witticisms, improbabilities, hyperbole and idiom," he said, and I pretended to understand what he was talking about. Then I asked him to speak English and use examples.

"Well," he wrote, "1 Kings 22 is filled with sarcasm. The apostle James had to be smiling when he wrote, in essence, 'You can tame every animal on earth, but not the tongue' (see James 3:7–8). And many of the Proverbs communicate timeless wisdom with a smile and a wink."

"But Arlene said Jesus didn't use humor."

"Who's Arlene?"

"Oh, just a girl who writes me four-page letters."

"Get a grip, Arlene. Jesus said, 'Why worry about the speck in your friend's eye when you have a log in your own?' Many of his parables are amusing cameos that the people loved and he usually had a quick response like, 'Let the dead bury their dead.' Jesus gave his disciples nicknames: Peter the Rock. James and John were hot-heads. He called them Sons of Thunder. He talked about people who gave out stones in place of bread, about the blind leading the blind, he called the holy men of his day 'whitewashed tombs.' How can you read the gospels without seeing the twinkle in his eye? He compares legalists with the guy who polishes the outside of his drinking cup but forgets to clean the inside, or picks a fly out of his drink and then swallows a camel. Sounds like a Pink Panther movie to me. You don't get invited to as many parties as he did by sucking on prunes all day. And he hung out with twelve guys. Do you really think they didn't laugh?"

I started to feel better and decided not to put my humor career on hold.

**Day 229.** In the Sunshine State, there was a car in front of us, driven by a leathery-faced lady who was at least ninety years young. A bumper sticker on the car stated: "Drink Coffee. Do stupid things faster with more energy."

Paul laughed. "Smoke cigarettes," he said. "Die younger with more cancer." Pretty good.

When we walked down the street, Paul noticed every cigarette that anyone was sucking on. "That's a long one!" "You can get them cheaper here!" "They sell those in packs of ten!" Do they have Smokeaholics Anonymous?

We ate at Gator's and I had...well, gator. Deep fried, breaded gator. Tasted like a twenty-three-year-old chicken that spent its life in an aquarium. Great conversation, though. No one asked how the gator tasted, so no lie was necessary.

**Day 230.** It's the night before we have to return to the cold north, so we formalized the adoption. To celebrate, we sat on a beach and watched the sun dip into the sea. I thought about suggesting that we smoke Cuban cigars to mark the occasion. I didn't mention it, though Paul told me he's through with smoking and that is celebration enough.

I'm all caught up on the Bible-reading program. It can be done.

**Day 232.** The news is on. Wonder what it would be like if the anchor came on and was honest enough to say, "You know, nothing horrible happened in our area all day. There was very little shoplifting at the mall, people were seen being kind to one another, nobody yelled or pushed, men were seen opening car doors for their wives."

I'd subscribe to a channel like that. But somehow, "whatsoever things are pure, honest, lovely, and of good report" didn't make it onto CNN tonight.[5]

**Day 233.** Today I was speaking at a men's conference. The guy who volunteered to drive me back to the airport wasn't dealing with a full deck. As we pulled onto the interstate, he said, "Did I tell you I died in a car accident once?"

We drove partly on the shoulder of the road as he told me the story. Then he excitedly proclaimed: "I have a ministry. I play the harmonica to passengers while I'm driving." (Help me, Lord!) He started fishing around under the seat for his blessed instrument, while I freaked out. I had no desire to die so far from home while riding in a car with a formerly dead, harmonica-playing driver.

I had no trouble being honest with him and immediately began to "pray without ceasing."[6]

"I'll find it. You drive," I insisted. "Please. Just drive."

Thankfully, the guy didn't ask me what I thought of his harmonica playing.

Note to self: Rent car next time.[7]

**Day 234.** Although I haven't withdrawn any cash from my blessed Internet account yet, I'm already beginning to consider the burdens that will undoubtedly accompany the onslaught of such great wealth. People will look at me differently. Friends will want to borrow money. Even fake friends will want to.

Will I use my time wisely once I quit my job? How will I avoid spoiling my children? Will they feel entitled? Will more money just make me more of what I already am? Will I suddenly become more generous, or will I remain slightly stingy, with a side order of greed? How will I remain thankful and dependent on God?

And what about my social life? Will I start hanging out with rich people? I've read that this happens when you're scratching with the big dogs.

I realize there are drawbacks to what's about to happen to me, but I'm up for it. Lord, here I am. Smite me with an influx of cash.

**Day 235.** I was speaking again tonight. The Queen's representative was planning to attend the event, at least that's what we were told. People were hungry and kept looking at their watches, probably placing wagers on how impossibly late he would be. My new eco-friendly watch was ticking fine. All it needs to keep going is a little sunlight.

The royal rep was almost an hour late, but that was okay. We needed the time to take a refresher course on how to act in his presence. Should his worship ever arrive and allow the hoi polloi to eat, we were to stand at attention while the musicians tried to drown out the rumbling of our stomachs with the first six bars of "God Save the Queen." From thenceforth we were not to approach him save through his loyal assistant. Neither shall there be snapping of pictures without said assistant's permission.

There also shalt be a general refraining from ill manners of any sort, loud clinking of forks, audible oinking, or any activities involving a wedgie. His worshipfulness shalt be the first served and the first to abscond his post. When he doth depart, we shalt stand in his presence and lightly applaud.

I must admit I'm not a person who waits patiently. God is working on me, but he's slow. I squirm a lot. I think of things I can do to get a rise out of the guards.

I love my British friends, and I think the Queen is a wonderful lady, but I am hungry and protocol like this has me thinking that if anyone so much as launches a tea bag into a pot of hot water, I'll be among the first of the rebels to top the hill, my musket ready.

**Day 236.** More speaking. Last night it was the stars, tonight it's the servants.

The flight is the bumpiest I've been on in years. Headwinds of four thousand miles an hour slap our Crash 8 (otherwise known as a Dash 8) about like a paper hat in Niagara. I'd gladly endure six days of it, though, just to meet the guys at this men's retreat. And to talk to Sam. Sam who says, "Hi, I'm Sam. I'm sorry for crying when you speak. I shouldn't cry."

"It's okay," I tell him. "My eyes leak sometimes too. Real men cry."

"Hi, I'm Sam," he repeats. "Was it wrong of me to take four sheets of toilet paper? He beat me for that. My dad hurt me for that."

*Ah, Sam.*

Someone told me Sam was beaten mercilessly by his father until the epileptic seizures began. Then he was kicked into the street. So the guys in the church took him in. They're his foster dads. One takes him to coffee, another to football games. One took him shopping and bought him a new suit. "Now I can be just like the rest of you," Sam says.

Sometimes I find myself wondering why I was born to Bernice and Victor Callaway, who smothered me with love and told me I was wonderful. I had nothing to do with it. It's not fair at all.

**Day 238.** I was hoping Paul's story would end where I last wrote about it, neat as a Disney movie—a former smoker puts away the cigarettes for good. But today my adopted son told me, "I only had one pack this week." And though I felt like jamming firecrackers up his remaining cigarettes, I was reminded of my daily shortcomings and the wonderful truth that I'm adopted too. My adoption as a son of God does not depend on my avoidance of failure, but on his unfailing love. So I gave Paul an enthusiastic high-five and reminded him that we're fellow pilgrims, he and I, stumbling heavenward.

Thanks to my visit with Paul earlier in the day, Mom was convinced that I'd been smoking. She sniffed loudly in the direction of my coat and shook her head. When I was ten, Mom caught me smoking a whole pack with a friend. I had wanted only two things from life that year: to eat a jar of dill pickles in one sitting and to smoke as many unfiltered cigarettes as I could get my lips around. I wanted to suck them in by the lung-full, blowing smoke rings through my nostrils. In those days smoking was good for you. "More doctors smoke Camels than any other cigarette," boasted a popular ad. Cigarettes were the oat bran of the sixties; they sold them even in health-food stores, I think. If they caught you not smoking in a mall, they made you stand outside twenty-five feet from the building.

I thought my mom would have a coronary, or at least have the good sense to ship me off to reform school. Instead, she leaned close and said, "Smoking won't send you to hell, son. It'll just make you smell like you've been there."

I don't pretend to understand the mystery of grace, but this eighty-five-year-old woman with dementia gave me a taste for it when I was ten. And I've gulped it greedily ever since. When I'm caught red-handed and run out of excuses, when I'm desperate and ashamed and wondering how God could save a wretch like me, grace comes along and lets me off the hook, leaving me breathless and grateful.

This year's truth assignment demonstrates how badly I need that grace. I need to soak in it like it's sunlight, and help others find it too.

## Honest Confession #8

We're commanded to weep with those who weep and rejoice with those who rejoice. Strange thing is, I have no trouble with the first part. I'm good at compassion, at bringing my wife's casseroles to the sick and grieving. Usually I do this without fanfare, hesitation, or complaint. And I listen well. As a result, people often introduce themselves to me and quickly relate the single worst event of their life. "I'm Frank, and my wife left me." This is a sacred trust, and I care and pray for these people.

But what about Rejoice with Those Who Rejoice 101? I'm flunking that class. When someone else enjoys tremendous success or sees their financial misfortunes take a turn for the better, I know I should celebrate. But envy is always lurking nearby.

# NINE

# A Thawing, Outside and In

They say that what happens in Vegas stays
in Vegas. It's a lie. The only thing that stays
in Vegas is your money.

JERRY SEINFELD

Always forgive your enemies. Nothing annoys
them so much.

—OSCAR WILDE

**D**ay 239. This morning our pastor quoted a great old preacher who started every sermon with a simple prayer: "Lord, if these people knew half of what you know about me, they wouldn't listen to a word I say." Not real catchy for a bracelet, but I know the feeling.

I wonder what people in this church would think if they knew I am in rehab for envy and a Pac-Man addiction, that I have developed severe allergies to vacuuming, and that my best intentions of reading the Bible through in a year are not panning out. The last few days

I've been wondering if anyone has published an Illustrated Modern English Abbreviated Version. I'd like that.

**Day 240.** I think I could forgive my traitor friend if he begged me for it. I'm ready. Bring it on. Maybe I could send him an anonymous note: "Apologize to Phil! I'll bet he'd forgive you." But I've heard that genuine forgiveness doesn't depend on him apologizing or even changing. Forgiveness is something that's done by the person who has suffered harm. There's nothing fair about this.

Reminds me of the time I told a friend, "Life isn't fair." He said, "Ya, but why can't it ever be unfair in my favor?"

**Day 241.** Outside, the snow is melting and there's progress inside of me as well. The prayers for my former friend, the one who is bent on destroying my reputation, have been thawing. For the first time, I have begun a slow, incremental journey toward caring for him.

A few months ago my prayer was, "Lord, dash his head against a rock, break his heart like he's broken mine, make his hair fall out." Mature stuff like that. But tonight I prayed, "Lord, give him heart palpitations, may his hair itch."

Clearly, I'm softening.

**Day 242.** I've been working out at our town's aquatic center three times a week, sometimes less if someone invites me to engage in something more enticing—like whacking my head with a rubber mallet.

I don't exercise because I enjoy it or because my wife threatens me if I don't. I exercise so that I can be a good steward of this earthly tent, which is the temple of the Holy Spirit. Actually, I can't lie. I exercise because a friend exercises with me and promises that we will do lunch afterward.

And I exercise because of Matilda.

Matilda (I've never asked her what her name is) glides effortlessly on the Trimline treadmill as I stagger to keep up on the Stair-

Master. I always listen to seventies music blasting from headphones and try hard to avoid looking like I am about to die. But not Matilda. She's model material. Her jet black hair is pulled back to reveal a flawless complexion, and even in January her legs are tanned like those of a Polynesian princess, not that I have noticed. I'll bet there are people who take comfort knowing that she's so thin, buzzards follow her home.

I don't ogle Matilda. Really. Never have. But I can't abide the thought that she would think of me as anything less than a guy in the prime of life. So I keep moving, smiling, pushing myself to exercise harder while trying not to die. I know I must be rupturing important organs, and fear that one day she will have to dial 911 on my behalf. How could I live with the embarrassment of having a heart attack in front of her?

This is shallow in every way, I know. Maybe borderline sinful. But for now it keeps me coming back to the aquatic center for more exercise. It keeps me moving in this cold, dark winter.

I wonder if Matilda has noticed my Florida tan? If I get up the nerve to talk with her, I may invite her to church

**Day 243.** Nothing happened. Really.

**Day 244.** From my office I called Ramona out of the blue and said, "Just wanted you to know that I love you."

She paused, expecting me to follow it up with something about me needing her to do me a favor. But I didn't, and both of us were impressed.

Later I drove the car six blocks to the exercise place so I could shed a few more calories. Matilda wasn't there, so I didn't worry about being impressive. Actually, I sat on the StairMaster reading an exercise magazine. It reminded me of my quiet times—great initiative; lousy follow-through. But Abraham never read the Bible; he just walked and talked with God. I tried it. With no one around, it was nice to be able to converse with the Lord out loud.

"God," I apologized, "I'm falling behind. Help me. I need a jump-start."

Suddenly I noticed Matilda was there. She's so fast and quiet, I hadn't noticed. I bet she heard everything. So now I'm not just old and out of shape, I'm Looney Tunes crazy.

**Day 246.** For some time now, I've been suspicious of a couple in our church whose children bear little resemblance to them. It doesn't trouble me except when they sit right in front of me in church. Like today. I couldn't concentrate on the sermon because I kept coming up with spicy scenarios.

Honestly, my brain seems to be a giant Ping-Pong ball. One minute I'm praising God, and the next I'm imagining that the mom sitting in front of me was previously married to a red-haired member of the IRA, or perhaps a Norseman named Erik. Her current husband sure doesn't fit the role.

Can I blame ADHD? I became a charter member in 1969.

Thankfully, the service ended with a time of quiet prayer so I could repent and ask God to give me strength for whatever wonderful things he has planned for me this week.

**Day 247.** Isaac, my investment guru, sounded like he was trembling when he called earlier today. "I hope you didn't invest more than you can afford to lose," he said.

"Say what?"

"There are rumors that this Internet-investment thing may not be entirely aboveboard."

My first reaction wasn't godly. By midnight I'd calmed down enough to tell God that if he gets me out of this, I'll give him 50 percent. FIFTY! How can he resist?

**Day 248.** Isaac again. He said I needed to check the investment Web site. So I booted up and found the notice: "This site has been closed due to illegal activity. A federal investigation is underway."

My heart sank down into my lungs. I said things to Isaac that I had to immediately apologize for.

I realized I have lost my shorts and my shirt. "Put yourself in my shoes," I told him. But I was exaggerating. My shoes are gone.

I ended the call and dialed Regi. He invested in the same scam, but didn't seem so troubled. Afterward, I smacked my fist way too hard against the Sheetrock wall. The noise I let out was not a joyful one. How come when they do this in movies, it doesn't seem to hurt?

**Day 249.** How to tell you've married a saint: Count how seldom she says, "I told you so." After you regain your senses, see if she says things like, "We'll be fine. It's okay. We'll have soup all month. I love you."

**Day 250.** It's not that hard to gain the rapt attention and abiding love of a few good friends. Just weave stories of your investment failings into conversations.

Tonight Vance, James, and I sat in a hot tub, where they were perfectly happy to just listen. In fact, they could scarcely contain their enthusiasm for hearing the entertaining tale of my misfortune. "Tell us about the time you invested in that big scam. Ha, ha, ha!"

I've been wondering about something. If this was God's money all along, and I was going to give it away anyway, can I write off the money I've lost as a tithe? If I could, that would take care of our charitable giving for years.

So I mentioned it to Ramona. She has slugged me only twice in our marriage.

I deserved it the first time too.

**Day 251.** Short list of things I've been whining about:
- losing money
- my left shoe pinching
- needing glasses

- grocery-store lines
- delays in airports
- erratic cell-phone reception
- my kids and their friends eating too much
- the burning out of the fridge's light bulb
- the stupid garbage truck always being late
- the snowstorm that blew in; front yard looks like the North Pole
- the dishwasher springing a leak—now a lake in my downstairs study that you could scuba-dive in

"It could be worse," said Ramona, flesh of my flesh.

"How could it be worse?"

In answer, she simply said: "Just count your blessings."

She was right, but I'm not saying so. If I were to start counting blessings, the list would be long. Start with a wife who rarely irritates me, a wife who still finds me mildly amusing. Kids who come for visits. A car that runs. A wristwatch that ticks.

And on Monday we depart for the Dominican Republic. I can't wait.

**Day 253.** Good news travels by mule where I come from. Bad news takes flight. People find out you've lost money and they want to share it with others so they can pray for you.

After church today, FG, a personal friend of Job, gripped my hand like a vice and told me that I lost all this money because I didn't have faith. Thankfully, I didn't say anything. Maybe he's right. Or maybe losing all this money was a blessing. Maybe I lost it because my faith was in the wrong place.

**Day 254.** At 4:30 a.m. Ramona and I left the 20-below icebox of Canada for the sand and surf of the Dominican Republic. This has been the coldest winter in thirty years where we live. The standard response to climate change in our town is, "Bring it on!"

8:04 a.m. Your luggage doesn't travel for free anymore, not on

US Airways. I asked the gal at check-in if my wallet is considered a carry-on and whether I'd have to fork over fifty dollars to bring it. I thought it was quite funny, but not to her. On this trip we're traveling with a group of pastors, so I'd better watch my words.

2:30 p.m. Paid two dollars for an in-flight Styrofoam cup of hot tea.

2:34 p.m. Asked for a refill, and I was asked for another two dollars. I insisted I'd use the old tea bag and needed only hot water. The flight attendant shook her head. Hot water costs two dollars.

I thought of things I could say, but Pastor Ed was right behind me. What if he heard me and issued a rebuke?

2:37 p.m. Heard Pastor Ed say, "WHAT? TWO DOLLARS! ARE YOU CRAZY?"

I brought along my crippled watch to give to someone. It really is a nice watch. You hold your head a little to the right and you can tell time.

**Day 255.** We're here to minister in some villages and see the work of Compassion, a child development agency. Quite honestly, I would prefer ten days on the beach reading thrillers. But I'm sure if I confide this to one of the pastors, he'll be disappointed in me. Except for Ed. He's human.

Our translator is Fernando, who learned to speak English watching American television. He prefaces his comments and observations with, "Oh my God!" which keeps us off balance. Reminds me of my Nashville friend Allan, whose four-year-old used those words the first time he saw snow. "We don't say that in conversation, son," scolded Allan. "Only when we're singing." So his four-year-old sang, "Oh my God, it's snowing."

The next time Fernando says this, I'll carefront him.

When he rings our room to call us for supper, he says, "Come on down! You're the next contestant on *The Price Is Right*."

**Day 256.** I was sweating by 8 a.m. and couldn't wait to e-mail the news to my friends back home. Poor suckers, huddling in their igloos praying for thicker mittens.

We're on Dominican time now, and there are two speeds: slow and stop. My favorite Dominican pastor is Saint Bernard, and although he has a very nice watch, he is time impaired. He assured us it was a half hour by bus to our first village. Three hours later, we arrived. I was cheerful, though. Really! I haven't been warm since November. Should have brought a dry shirt, though. Walking down the sidewalk is like dancing on lava.

First stop, Jose's house. Jose works for the army. Seventy-five percent of his salary goes to pay the rent on a tarpaper shack the size of my garden shed. An aloe plant stands guard above his door, bravely warding off evil spirits. I talked with him through Bernard, about the power of *Diablo* and the knockout punch of *Cristo*.

Jose's wife handed their darling daughter to her husband and retrieved her Bible from behind a blanket curtain. I showed Jose some verses. "He wants to pray with you," said Bernard, as if this is a perfectly normal activity. "He wants to follow Jesus now."

"What?"

Oh me of little faith.

On the bus someone asked me why I was carrying an aloe plant. Jose gave it to me to throw away. He doesn't need it anymore.

**Day 257.** By 3 p.m. in another village, we ran into a little problem. Lorena was translating for us, and after we dropped off boxes of food, four men picked up our trail.

"This is no good," said Lorena, her head down. "Let's keep moving; they want money. This is a bad area. Very bad."

I didn't think I could walk so fast. "Let me call Bernard," I suggested, puffing a bit. "He has the bus. I'll get him to come right away."

"Bernard, yes, we need you here. There are guys following us and they...um...want money. It's not good. Lorena says it's very bad... Can you come?"

"Is Jesus with you?"

"Uh…yes…um…Jesus is with us, Bernard. But what I'd really like to see right now is a bus!"

4 p.m. We're alive! The men were too drunk to outwalk us!

6 p.m. Dinner menu is chicken feet and rice. Fernando rescued me. "My grandparents were slaves. They lived on chicken feet. Here. You eat the meat. Homer Simpson eats anything, no?"

"Gracias, Fernando."

9 p.m. Ramona came over for a cuddle, but my skin was a raging inferno.

"Ouch!"

"Why didn't you use sunscreen?"

"Oh…I, well I —"

"Come on, you're supposed to tell the truth, remember?"

"I want my friends back home to be envious of my tan."

**Day 258.** Pastor Rod greeted me before breakfast with a firm slap to the back and a vigorous, "This is the day that the Lord has made, brother."

I thought of some words I've learned from watching American television, but managed a warm, albeit high-pitched "Good morning." Not to throw cold water on things, but my back is a tad tender and looks like raw steak. I recalled the words of Proverbs 27:14, "He that blesseth his friend with a loud voice, rising early in the morning, it shall be counted a curse to him." I decided to share it with Rod.

Sun-damaged or not, I managed to keep my chin up. Back home in Canada, it's three thirty in the morning. My poor sucker friends are asleep, their feet nuzzled up against warm rocks.

After breakfast we visited a project where fifty unmarried teenage moms are being mentored and cared for and taught a trade. Bernard's friend Albert is paying the ticket. He's a well-known baseball player and, according to ESPN, makes $13,870,949 a year.

Wish I could do something to help with the needs here. If only that stupid investment had panned out. Must admit that part of the thrill would be having people talk about how generous I am. I've walked with Jesus all these years, but I'm so clumsy. I guess C. S. Lewis was right, I've never had a selfless thought since I was born.

A little girl at the project thought I was a faith healer. She took my hand and begged me to come pray for her little brother. We walked over cobbled streets where boys were playing baseball with sticks and empty shampoo bottles. Inside a cardboard house, the little brother lay on a dirty mat, his crippled legs beneath him, while Mama scurried about trying to make the place presentable. Not a scrap of food in sight. No husband. No hope.

I took the little guy in my arms, and I couldn't stop crying. I prayed for his legs. For his mama and his sister. I prayed for mercy, for hope. And I prayed for me too: "Oh, God, what can I do? I'm just one little guy." And I knew exactly what to do.

We found a store and filled two shopping carts with flour and beans and rice and sugar and things kids love. We took it to the cardboard house and celebrated Christmas and Easter all at once, in a home where no one whines about slow grocery-store lines or shoes that pinch. There was only this moment of giving thanks for fistfuls of rice and chocolate bars, and perhaps a little more hope than there had been a few hours earlier.

**Day 259.** The last few days of the trip we're spending at a resort. Pastor Rod calls it "suffering for Jesus." We can choose from five restaurants. All you can eat. All you can drink. Not a lot of people dieting here. Some, including me, likely should.

A mile away, people are foraging in garbage bins. At the resort, people sit by the pool, oblivious to the scenery and surf, downing shrimp and staring at a rum and Coke through cloudy eyes. Rich and poor, we're pretty much the same. Drowning out the hollowness inside.

A guy on the beach offered me a box of genuine Cuban cigars for twenty dollars. "I could bring them home for Paul," I told Ramona. I was joking, of course. She said, "You smoke one of those things, you can sleep in Cuba."

It seems many of the women at the resort are impoverished European tourists who can't afford tops for their swimsuits. I decide we should take up a collection for them. If I mention this to the pastors, will they be surprised? I bet none of them has even noticed.

One of the clergy is wearing sunglasses to shield his eyes from the sun. Maybe I should ask him.

Fernando asked why I call Ramona "Mony."

"Why?" I said. "What does it mean in Spanish?"

"Wife of a monkey," he says. "Oh my G—."

I wanted to give him something, and all I had was the watch with a cockeyed face. Plus the one I was wearing on my wrist. I think it says in the Bible that you can't give away a Christmas gift from your wife, so at dinnertime I handed him my crooked old watch that is limping its way to 8 p.m. Thankfully, it was growing dark outside. He couldn't see the face.

We sat up late talking and praying for the people we'd met. There were lots of tears. I don't think we'll ever be the same.

A few of the pastors admitted there was a scarcity of complete swimsuits here. Aha! They're human too.

"I'm shocked you noticed," I found myself saying, with a straight face.

**Day 260.** Our last day here in the Dominican Republic. Carlos, a kid that Ramona and I have sponsored through Compassion for ten years, joined us at the grand resort. His eyes bugged out of his head. We played catch in the pool and ate more than we could lift.

I told him through a translator that we don't live this way back home, and we sure don't eat like this. He laughed as if he agreed with me. But secretly I bet he was thinking: *You're millionaires. You have shoes.*

"We leave here tomorrow, but we hope to see you again, Carlos. And if we don't, there's a great feast coming that will make this one look like a dog's breakfast." I told him about heaven, how God is preparing a place for him. He bent over and wrote in the sand: "Carlos Ramona Philippe." Then he drew a cross. Shoot. Here came the tears again.

The translator was confused. "Dog's breakfast?" he said.

**Day 261.** I considered whining about my fatigue and the length of the flight, but didn't. I didn't even whine when I had to pay for my luggage, or when I paid two dollars for another cup of tea. Ramona was noticeably impressed.

"If ever I whine again, whap me upside the head with a salami from our dark refrigerator."

**Day 262.** Went to Costco where I bought a watch like mine—one with the "12" to the north—and couriered it to our translator in the DR. In the hopes of helping him think of eternal things you won't find on American television, I attached a note that read: "My friend, Fernando. One day this watch will stop. Then I'll see you in heaven."

Later I thought about the wording, long after the package had been shipped. Hope he doesn't view it as a threat.

**Day 263.** First mistake today was walking the dog and bumping into a woman whose cat has been missing for a few days. She was in a foul mood. Second mistake was saying, "Dogs come when you call; cats take a message and get back to you later." I meant it as a joke to help propel her forward to a sunshiny day filled with laughter and joy, but something got lost in translation. I dug a little deeper: "No one owns a cat."

My dog smelled four-day-old cat scent on the woman and growled, so that didn't help. I felt so bad, I offered to help look for the cat. Third mistake.

Soon I was walking our neighborhood with a Shih Tzu, yelling, "Here, Garfield, here kitty, kitty, kitty."

My neighbor friend Andrew popped his head over the hedge and asked, "You okay?"

Not sure which is worse, guilt or humiliation.

"Why would you name a cat?" he asked.

"I didn't."

"We had a cat once. We called it a nuisance." Andrew is not a fan of cats and has his own quotes to back up his sentiments. "Dogs believe they are human," he said. "Cats believe they are God."

**Day 264.** Dear God:

Maybe it's the honesty thing, but I need to say that I've been steamed at you all day. I know you already know this, but I need to write it down.

Can you explain why you had to allow my brother-in-law Lauren to get bone cancer? He's one of your handpicked saints and my dear friend these past twenty-five years. Discouraged people drive an hour just to shake his hand, like they're an electric car in need of a plug-in. Lauren and I have vacationed together, golfed, painted, laid bricks, fixed toilets, and hung wallpaper—any of these activities can ruin the most sturdy of friendships. Why him? I know cancer falls on the just and the unjust, but why not make an exception and inflict his upon one of the unjust? I can come up with a list of people, if you need one.

And then there's his son—my nephew. Why'd he have to get it too? And now his son's wife has a tumor. Their three little kids need their parents.

While we're on the subject, I've never been much good at understanding why my wife has seizures, and why my mom can't talk English when I visit her. But what really tightened my shorts today was that one of your kids told me I have no business being ticked at you. Mostly I think of brilliant answers about two days later. But I told him that Jacob and Moses and Abraham and Job went toe to toe with you...and lived. He smiled real smug and said, "You need to give it over to God. Let go and let God. What are you doing under the circumstances? Have faith."

I decided not to murder him. I'm refraining from violence not so much because it would violate one of your commandments, but because I do not want to serve jail time. I know this isn't very spiritual of me.

I'm sorry.

I love you, but I have trouble understanding you.

Your servant,

Phil

**Day 266.** Can't get that guy's words out of my mind: "Let go and let God." I know there's truth in most clichés. I'm willing to accept that guys like this may make it to heaven. But I'm reasonably certain that they will spend eternity at the trumpet recitals of other people's children.

### Honest Confession #9

I am a lapsed Pharisee, so who am I to judge others? But sometimes Christians drive me nuts. I am not a Christian because I follow people who follow Jesus. I follow Jesus himself. Many of my friends who have stopped attending church have confided that what drove them away was the unkindness of fellow believers, often expressed through gossip. I can't describe how sad this makes me and how determined I am to be part of the solution, which I think has partly to do with staying in church with the other 93 percent of fabulous people, doing my part to pull out the welcome mat, smack some backs, and burp some babies.

# TEN

# My Judgment Day

The rope of a lie is short.

— ARABIAN PROVERB

If you judge people, you have no time to love them.

—MOTHER TERESA OF CALCUTTA

**Day 267.** Everything in church convicted me this morning. The songs we sang ("How Deep the Father's Love for Us"), the people around me (Kevin Penner, with his daughter in a wheelchair and his hands open to God), and the couple in front of me (with the red-headed kids). Turns out the kids did have a different father, since they are adopted.

If we had ballots for sainthood, I'd drop the names of these parents in the offering plate.

FG, best buddy of Job, greeted me on the way out.

"Take care," I said, with a wave and smile.

"No," he corrected. "We don't take care. We cast all our cares upon him."

"Doh."

My neighbor Andrew saw me pull into the driveway and had another cat joke. "Cats are smarter than dogs. Have you ever seen eight cats pulling a sled through snow?"

**Day 268.** I got stuck in traffic with the radio playing "'Cause I'm a picker, I'm a grinner, I'm a lover, and I'm a sinner."[2] On the back of the car in front of me, there was a fish symbol, plus a bumper sticker that announced: "God is my copilot." Really? He's in the passenger seat offering suggestions? Maybe you should give him the wheel.

**Day 269.** Incredible answer to prayer today!

Bernie Madoff's self-proclaimed wife, Ruth,[3] e-mailed me from a hospital somewhere. Me! With her Ponzi-scheme husband jailed for the next one hundred fifty years, and a judge freezing her assets, it appears she fled the country. Thankfully, she claimed, her husband had the foresight to deposit millions of dollars of other people's money in her name with a finance firm in Europe. All she needed was for me to run it through my bank account, keep some of it, and send the rest back to her! She's a "born again Christian," she wrote, and signed off with "God bless ou!"

The e-mail sender, "Ruth Madoff," is not a great speller, but that's a small matter. She chose me!

I set up a special e-mail account and sent an immediate response:

SUBJECT: Wow!

Dear Ruth,

Just let me know how I can help. This money will be used wisely, you can count on me.

PS: Will your husband get early parole? Can we get some of this money to him, so he can use it to start up a business or something?

**Day 270.** Today Lauren and I headed north where I'll be speaking. Then we'll backtrack two thousand miles to the south. Lauren is exhausted from a week of medical tests on his hindquarters and is reeling from news of the Big C. Before we left, I asked if he was sure he wanted to go on this trip. He joked, "It's not like it'll make things worse."

He puts a brave face to it, but this is nasty stuff that has spread like a grease fire. He didn't know what hit him until the pain began.

Last weekend his pastor asked him to update the church family on his health. He started out, "Some of you have asked me what you can do for me now that I have cancer. Just be a whole lot nicer, that's all."

I'm not sure what to say, so mostly I listen. And pray. "Lord, you can't take him. Give his cancer to a terrorist or those guys who start computer viruses. You can do it."

**Day 271.** At the airport Lauren and I bought sandwiches and asked for seats closer to the front of the aircraft. Any chance to de-plane thirty seconds earlier, I'll seize it. The flight attendant recognized me as an author. We talked for a few minutes, she said she'd see what she could do, then handed us tickets for Row 3.

First class!

Printed dinner menu!

Choice of thirty thousand movies!

Massage chairs you can lose small animals in!

We hid our sandwich bags under the seat, then ordered a roast with steamed veggies and dessert that could be smelled all the way back in Row 42.

"Um...Lord, it's me again. I don't understand much. I'm so small. But thanks for moments like these along the way."

Beside me sat Lauren. He doesn't have a clue about tomorrow, but for now he is sitting in first class; eating a side of beef; fiddling with massage buttons; and grinning like a four-year-old, baseball-loving kid who just heard a rumor that his father owns the New York Yankees.

"One hundred percent of us die," he told me on the way to the hotel. "We're all terminal."

We watched a few minutes of the severely juvenile film that I'm careful to never recommend to anyone, *Dumb and Dumber,* and laughed until we fell off our beds.

Things are that much funnier when you haven't slept in a week.

**Day 272.** I'm starting to think that my long-distance correspondent, "Ruth Madoff," doesn't check her e-mail much. Or maybe I didn't sound sincere enough when I replied to her generous offer. Imagine that.

**Day 273.** My son Jeff and his friend Calvin visited today, and though Calvin is in college and is a brilliant mathematician and a prolific eater, the poor kid can't speak conversational English in a group larger than two. It must be hard on his parents. It's killing me.

Jeff and Calvin were conversing while I attempted to make supper. In less than four minutes, I counted thirty-two instances of this normally clever kid butchering the word *like.*

"You know like I bet like our team can like get through like to like the finals if we like just like give it, you know?" It's a trendy tic this generation has developed and spread like a virus.

I said, "So like do you like think like you'd like like pepperoni like on this you know like pickin' pizza?"

Calvin frowned at me as if my delivery needed some work.

**Day 274.** The sermon today was about loving your enemies, blessing those who curse you, doing good to those who hate you, and praying when someone despitefully uses you. Apart from my most committed enemy—the one who has spread buckets of guck about me—it's not like I've gathered a lot of enemies in my travels. I sometimes receive mail from angry people who think laughter is out of

place in the Christian life, like allergies at a dog show. And there are
a few folk who scratch my blackboard if I let them, but mostly I enjoy
good relationships built on kindness and the fact that we don't live
next door to one another or vacation together.

When I was a kid, Cary Pauls was the closest thing I had to a
real, live enemy. One time he drilled me between the shoulder blades
with a homemade javelin from sixty feet, then mocked me for almost
dying. But that was forty years ago, and I don't know where he lives
now. I suppose I could do an Internet search so I could carefront him
on it, but I harbor no bitterness and genuinely hope he's doing well.
Guys are like that, I suppose. Some of my best friends today are those
who pounded on my pointy little head during recess. Without a
doubt, I deserved it.

At this stage in my life, most of the adversarial offensives are
launched from afar, like this note I received a few weeks ago:

> In one of your novels, a boy takes the wings off a fly. I think
> you did that when you were a child, didn't you? I think you
> took great pleasure in it. I want you to know that I tore your
> book into the smallest pieces I could and put it in the waste-
> basket. You need psychological counseling. You are sick, sick,
> sick.

The reason I kept the note and have considered bronzing and
framing it is that it was written on a beautiful card graced with blue-
birds and a Bible verse that says, "Under his wings you will find refuge;
his faithfulness will be your shield and rampart" (Psalm 91:4, NIV).

I wonder if the writer spent extra time finding a card with that
particular verse. I would love to ask her about it, if only she had in-
cluded her address and signed more than her first name: Grace. Ah,
the irony.

But back to today's sermon. Is God speaking to me? I think so.

**Day 275.** Tonight I found myself behind the wheel of a Porsche Carrera, and the worst thing about it was that it's Mark's, not mine. Another friend claims that the best way to find out if you're too attached to something is to give it away. I suggested this to Mark, but no luck. These things are fast. They are built to get you from point A to point B in the fastest possible time with the least possible whiplash, like an electron zinging around an atom.

Thought I'd drive really fast and give my wife goose bumps. Instead, she got motion sickness.

"Why don't I have more stuff?" I whined.

"That's really good," Ramona said. "Compare yourself to 1 percent of the world and forget about the other ninety-nine."

She wasn't feeling well when she said this, so I forgave her. Sounded like she's taken a truth vow.

"Please speak a little more respectfully," I said with a grin. "Women in the Old Testament addressed their husbands as 'lord.'"

**Day 276.** I checked "Ruth Madoff's" initial e-mail again. There is no phone number, which is too bad. Sure could use some cash.

So I e-mailed her again:

SUBJECT: Just wondering…

Dear Ruth,

I received your urgent e-mail and responded to it, but haven't heard back. Are you all right? I hope everything is okay. Just let me know if you'd like my phone number or what. I just want to help. I can't believe you chose me. Why?

Phil

**Day 277.** Dementia has robbed the pictures from a scrapbook Mom spent her entire life pasting together. Sometimes I'm angry

about this. I'm angry that I've had to say good-bye to her in install-
ments. That although she's here, we haven't been able to have a ra-
tional two-way conversation in a long time.

"Lord, is she okay? Where is her mind when she's incoherent?
She's served you for decades, why this? Please hold her close."

Then I'm reminded that, for the most part, she's been pretty
happy the last year. Mom has suffered much through life, things she
wouldn't talk about until her sixties. And tonight there she was, smiling at me without any reason for it. Telling me how she played with
her dollies today. And snuggling with a bear I brought her. She's
blissfully happy. I'm the one with all the questions.

**Day 278.** On the road again. I flagged down a taxi around noon
and practiced one of my most successful methods of sharing my
faith. It's borderline sneaky, ethically suspect, possibly illegal in some
states and provinces.

Here's how it works. I get in a cab and start reading C. S. Lewis's
*Mere Christianity*, holding it in such a way that the bored Muslim
taxi driver swivels his neck trying to figure out what it is.

"Oh," I say, with feigned surprise. "This is an amazing book.
Have you ever heard of C. S. Lewis? You know, the Narnia movies?
Brilliant man. An atheist, you know. Then he became a follower of
Jesus. He believed that we can't earn salvation, that it is by grace we
are saved, through faith. What do you think?"

Bringing your dog with you is a great conversation starter, but
sometimes a book must suffice. Today I had a long talk about Jesus
with a kind cab driver. Bummer that he left the meter running, so I
had to cut it short. I climbed out and left him a generous tip. "Oh, I
have an extra copy of the book," I said. "Do you want one?"

He reached out his hand.

"You have to give the tip back," I said. "Just joking."

I handed him the book.

The last guy told me to take a hike, but when you're this bold, there will be persecution.

No real converts to show yet, but you never know.

**Day 279.** I continue to let my light shine before men. And women. When I'm in a hotel, I have taken to opening the Gideon Bible and leaving it on the nightstand with a couple-dollar tip and a note that says, "This is amazing! Take a minute to read chapter 4! Thanks!"

Should I leave an e-mail address so I can keep track of converts?

I was interviewed on television today, though my face was created for radio. The hosts were a high-haired couple with a worldwide ministry. In the green room they were disagreeing about something I didn't understand and casting lethal glances at each other.

He paced and practiced a few words in front of a massive mirror. I wouldn't believe it if I hadn't seen it. "Gaaaalloorrry!" "Euuuniteeaaauu."

I had no idea those words had so many syllables.

**Day 281.** Lately my favorite prayer is "HELP!" And then today came along, and my favorite prayer became "THANK YOU!"

I was speaking at the closing rally of a women's conference. There were five hundred women there, and apart from the sound man, I was the only male in attendance. A photographer got really close to take pictures. I said, "I'm having hot flashes." The audience found that funnier than I thought they would.

A man in his midthirties entered the room and sat at the very back, hunched over to avoid detection. After the service he told me that he had been taking notes. "I play in the bar band here at the hotel. I couldn't sleep this morning, so I was walking around. I heard laughter. I couldn't believe you were a bunch of Christians. Imagine. Christians laughing."

I smiled at him.

"My parents in Boston have been praying for me since I was a kid. God heard their prayers today. Thanks."

I was so excited that I left for the airport, forgetting a great host of things, including a few of my favorite CDs.

**Day 282.** Today was wrinkle free, one of those days you're only allowed to dream about. Two of our children arrived home just to hang out; they didn't even need their laundry done. A national women's magazine called wanting to run my column, and an e-mail arrived complimenting me on the behavior of my son in college. That had never happened before in the history of e-mail.

A record snowfall arrived too, and frost coated the trees. That created a picture-postcard view out each window. My son managed to purchase a new used car, and I helped him winterize it. As we snacked on ice cream at midnight, he said he wants to work with youth and tell them about Jesus. The dog was at our feet making jerking motions in her sleep. I had to pinch myself. Does life get better? Maybe. Next week is the DVD shoot and two sold-out evenings for my talks on laughter. Can't wait.

**Day 283.** When my son Jeff was ten, he had some hooligan friends over, and one of them blasted a golf ball through the glass doors of my study. Shards are still stuck in one wall as mementos. Today Jeff was wearing the same expression he had on that day as he pointed with his nose to the stairway. I descend slowly like it was the climax of a horror movie.

"Mom went out," I heard him say.

Halfway down, my nose wrinkled. I'll spare you the details in case you're reading this during lunch, but clearly our sewer had backed up. It wasn't the first time, so I knew the drill. Don mask. Grab shovel. Carry bucket. Swirl mop. Repeat three hundred times while muttering, "Dog biscuits!"

I tried to remember the beauty of the snow-scene postcards outside, but it's tough to remember much when your eyes keep watering and you can't breathe.

Later I relapsed on Pac-Man. Figured I owed it to myself.

**Day 284.** The plumber arrived before breakfast and spent an hour fiddling with assorted pipes downstairs. I stayed in the kitchen. Afterward, I gave his bill a careful examination. Then I asked God why I never received a call to go into plumbing.

**Day 285.** Finally! An e-mail from "Ruth Madoff." She was sorry for taking so long, explaining that she had been sick. She attached a picture of herself in a hospital bed, though only the back of her head is visible. She's a really bad speller and the grammar is atrocious, but when someone's sending you this much money, it's no time to get picky.

> SUBJECT: PLEASE DO TO GETTING BACK TO ME
>
> Dear Beloved Phill,
>
> God blesses you and thanked you for mail. I am very grateful for the interest shown in my polite and want to assure you that God will reward you and why you has chosen. I have strong feeling that you are the chosen for this greet mission. Then I prayed and fastened and believed my relevation. The good Lord directioned me as I prayed and searched Internet and God makes not misteaks. I have $25,142,728.00 in a bank in Europe awaiting my disbursable. My doctor say I would not last eight months due to sick. My husband's relatives are not Christians and would use this money for worldlies. They are waiting to hear that I am dead so that they lay hands on my last belongs. I do not want them to know about us. That is for how I am commuting with you. Please assure me you will keep this conferential and will contact the finance firm and the release of the finds. I will also want to know about your spiritual life. I do not know when my tim will be up. I require your urgent respond so that my lawyer can make you beneficial.
>
> Your Sister,
> Ruth Madoff

**Day 286.** I'm so excited I can hardly type without my eye twitching.

SUBJECT: Wow! Wow! Wow!
Dear Ruth,

I am blown away about this and have so many questions. I know you wanted me to keep this confidential, but I couldn't help it. I told a close friend and he was skeptical, but he already asked me for money. I told him, "NO WAY! YOU'RE FREAKING ME OUT!" I think I would be a good guy to take care of your money, but I'm worried it might ruin me. I've seen people win the lottery and—*boom!*—their lives and marriages go up in smoke and they want cars and boats and stuff, stuff, stuff! They're never happy. And friends and family want it all.

I think I have a strong resolve, but what if? I would like to think I would use the money wisely for the Lord's work, because everything we have is God's (as you know), but what happens if I go on a binge and start drinking or the pride of it all just goes to my head or something? Down deep I really, really want to do what is right, but I am concerned about our Lord's caution against serving God and Mammon. Can I really do it? I've never had much money, so I don't really know.

Do you still want to risk things with a guy like me? You're not well, so I hate to give you any more grief. Maybe you should give it to someone more worthy of trust. There's still time for you to back out.

Just wondering,
Phil

**Day 287.** Received a reply to my last e-mail.

Dear Beloved Phil,

I completely understand how skepticed you may be about my offer on the fat that I have not really met with you before or knowed you all my life. But though I have not with you person, I still have believed my faith and so am confadance that you are the Chosen one. I give you my word that you will be rewarded accordably and you will not regret to live any bit of this mission you are to accomplish. As a result of fraudulent activist going on all over the, we do not know who to trust, but I strongly think you are honest and God fearing. Please do not let me down as I do not know when my time will up.

Your Sister,

Ruth Madoff

**Day 288.** Our beloved minister dropped all sensitivity in favor of going straight for my jugular this morning. I feel like a dog with its head out the window, my ears pinned back. He talked of Dietrich Bonhoeffer, the German pastor who was arrested and executed for his involvement in a plot to assassinate Adolph Hitler. Bonhoeffer wrote, "Anybody who has once been horrified by the dreadfulness of his own sin that nailed Jesus to the Cross will no longer be horrified by even the rankest sins of a brother."[4]

The ADHD had me hearing only brief snippets from a forty-two-minute sermon and fixating on them. Sometimes this is good. I think of my need to forgive. Probably the most frightening truth I'm encountering this year is the fact that seemingly good and ordinary people like me are capable of heinous thoughts, and if not checked, the worst kinds of evil. It's in us all.

Not exactly the kind of uplifting stuff I was hoping for at church, but sometimes the truth is not therapy.

When it comes to loving others, I am a baby Christian. I am in the nursery hoping to graduate to the Pablum stage. But when it comes to judging others, I'm an authority. I have my doctorate. I am buff, robust, mature, in the prime of life. I can spot phonies and Pharisees and pick them off at five hundred yards, but I'm not so good at looking in the mirror.

Forgive me, Lord.

**Day 289.** I came to my senses and unloaded on Ramona about my former friend who continues to do his level best to destroy me. Yesterday's sermon aside, I have been wronged.

She said, "Jesus died for him too." I stomped around for an hour or two, fiddling and fuming.

Tonight I prayed for the former friend. "God, I don't get it. I never will. But you created him, so maybe you can change him… even though he doesn't deserve it, and I kind of wish you wouldn't."

**Day 290.** Don't ask me why, but I decide to keep the e-mails going with "Ruth Madoff." Yes, I am way outside my truth vow, but I have a purpose for the e-mail correspondence. Plus, they're kind of fun.

> Dear Ruth,
>
> Woo-hoo! My head is still spinning and my eyes can hardly focus. This is amazing! You still want me! I know exactly what to do to make it easier for us both. I will fly to visit you in the hospital. Jesus said, "I was sick and you visited me," so my wife has given me the okay! Woo-hoo! Just let me know where you are, and I am hoping to come and be a blessing to you there.
>
> When I visit the sick in hospitals, I read some scriptures and pray that the sick will have comfort and maybe be healed, so you never know. Wouldn't that BE SOMETHING? You and me JUMPING AROUND THE HOSPITAL? I want you to know that if you are healed, you can just keep ALL THE MONEY. (Unless you want to reimburse my plane ticket; that

would be okay.) Just let me know what airport I should fly into, and I will take care of the expenses. We will be able to work things out better that way too, won't we?

Excitedly,

Phil

PS: It must be hard for you to write such lengthy e-mails when you aren't feeling well. You look so ill in your picture.

**Day 291.** We were on our way to the airport (not to see Ruth) and my cell phone started playing "Sweet Home Alabama." It was a guy at Visa who asked if I'd put through a $9,100 charge to an exotic online pet store. I said, "Just a minute... Honey, did you buy a llama... Are you kidding me?"

"We didn't think so," said Mr. Visa. "It doesn't track with your spending habits."

"What kind of pets can you buy for $9,100?" I wondered out loud. "Can you get a giraffe?" He didn't know the answer, but my card had been cancelled, and the guy said they would reissue one. We should have it in a week.

"I'm on the way to the airport," I said, way too loudly. "I have to rent a car today, stay in a hotel, eat out."

"Um...okay, when you get to the rental desk, you call this number. We'll open your account for a brief moment, then close it."

"And at restaurants?"

"Just do the same thing."

Oh great.

It was raining small horses when we touched down. In the hotel, I flipped on my computer but nothing happened. All that showed up was the Blue Screen of Death. Tomorrow I am to speak in front of five hundred people and four high-definition cameras for ninety minutes in a swanky theater. This is my big DVD taping, and I was hoping to go over my notes ahead of time.

"What if the stress of all this makes me panic and I run from the stage?" I asked Ramona.

"Well, it could be a big hit on YouTube," she said, flipping out the light. It was eleven o'clock on the nose. I could see my watch clearly. It was lit up by a big blue screen.

**Day 292.** The rain turned to ice and was soon covered by eight inches of snow. On that kind of surface, you slip easily but you land soft. I managed to cram the sixty-minute drive to the theater into three hours. Lola, my GPS lady, kept leading me down wrong roads—then recalculating. Once she had us turning into a farmer's field. We slid all the way to the hall, but finally made it.

Rehearsal was flawless. Cameras were all working well. Great acoustics. Great atmosphere.

We prayed in the green room (which was blue). Peace for me, a blessing for the audience, excellence on all the technical stuff.

I was shown the DVD cover for "Learning to Laugh When Life Stinks." It was all done but the recording.

An hour into the recording, I knew something was wrong.

"Sound trouble," said the technician during intermission. "The picture looks great, though. This high def is somethin'."

**Day 293.** I was back home when Chad from the tech crew called. The video shoot is unusable. Mondo moola down the drain.

My son's friend Calvin wasn't helping my mood. "So I was like, you know like totally, and she was like whatever, so I was like yah, like don't you like get it? And she was like…"

It wasn't the right time to get involved, but I asked Calvin: "Did you ever hear someone scrape their fingernails on a blackboard?"

Jeff and Calvin stopped conversing and looked my way.

"Calvin, here's five bucks. It's yours if you can talk for two minutes without using the word *like* improperly."

He snatched the money.

I'm afraid that with all this writing about being truthful, I might snap one of these days and start yelling like a football coach, maybe throw a spaghetti spoon at one of the kids.

My prayer has changed from "Help" to "Thanks" to more basic stuff like, "Lord, help me not strangle someone today. Help me stay out of jail."

The truth is, I like the next generation. I really do. But I hate that they sound like cavemen: Ugh…ugh…fire…ugh…like ugh.

Less than a minute later, Calvin handed me back my five dollars. The way things are looking, I'm gonna need it.

**Day 294.** I'm at it again with judging people, even complete strangers. We stopped for lunch in a crowded cafeteria. Only one table was empty, save for a mess of dirty plates and four scattered nickels. I was tired, so I sat down, wondering who would leave such a mess. A mother came over and apologized, saying her son had left the table to go wash up.

"Oh, I'm sorry," I said.

"No, you go ahead and sit there."

Out of the rest room came the cutest little kid, walking on tiny crutches. He retrieved the nickels, then plunked them one by one into a wishing well to help kids with cystic fibrosis.

"Um, thanks for the table," I stammered. "Here…uh…add these."

**Day 295.** Job's buddy FG was at church again today. You might recall he's the one who maintains I lost my money because of a lack of faith. He heard about the fiasco of the failed DVD taping, and said the devil didn't want anyone to see my performance and that's why the audio malfunctioned. He clarified that my recorded performance would have blessed too many people, so Satan thwarted it.

I appreciated the compliment, but I'm not buying it. I did find it odd, however, that the greatest performance of my life can be seen and not heard. It's like hitting a hole in one with no one around to witness it. Maybe we could add subtitles. I could be like Buster Keaton in one of those grainy, jerky, pretalkie movies.

**Day 297.** I checked the online pet store. Sure enough. You can buy a giraffe. But not for $9,100. The guy must have been trying to purchase a shark for his pool. Oh, I also got a new e-mail from "Ruth Madoff":

> Dear Beloved Phil,
>
> I thank you and also your courage and commencement. I reside in Kuwait. I am formerly an ark teacher. Presently I am in New Dar Al-Shifa Hospital where my set time is to end. I must confess also that I am not in a very sound statue at the moment as a result for my present ailment, and am going through severed pans. Based on this reasonable, please do not visit, this trouble would much too that you have to come here.
>
> Yours Truly,
>
> Ruth

## Honest Confession #10

I am so often a phony. And my automatic reaction to this realization is to vow to turn over a new leaf and try harder. It doesn't work. My pastor says that Jesus wants everything. He says if we hand over the whole tamale—the sin, the desires, and the good stuff too—in exchange, we get a new self. We don't simply change our behavior; we reorient our life around God. Augustine said that if there is a God who created me, then the deepest chambers of my soul can't be filled up by anything else. I've been too full of myself to allow God to fill me. Sorry, Lord. It's all yours.

# ELEVEN

# Up and Away

Men occasionally stumble over the truth, but
most of them pick themselves up and hurry off
as if nothing had happened.

—WINSTON CHURCHILL

Faith opened doors for my mind and my life
that I could have never before imagined.
Walking with God has broadened, not narrowed,
my base of knowledge and experience.

—ALICIA BRITT CHOLE, FORMER ATHEIST

**D**ay 298. I awakened this morning, thought of my enemy friend
(the gossip), and prayed: "Lord, you forgave people who wounded
you with whips and nails; maybe I should get on with forgiving
him."

I have no idea where this came from. From God, you think?

**Day 299.** I've had a nagging feeling of guilt about the notes I
sent to "Ruth Madoff," so I've decided to bring the correspondence
to an abrupt conclusion with only a few more e-mails.

Dear Ruth,

You urged me to not come visit you, but I don't want you to worry about a thing. This is all SO EXCITING! Last night I bought a ticket on Kuwait Airways flight 1509, arriving into Kuwait City just after midnight. How exciting is THAT? Just so you're not worried, I did get a great last-minute price of just over $2,100 (I fly economy), and my wife agreed to it. (We do have a little money that we had put away for retirement after all those years in the pastor-ate.) I will not visit you until a week from this coming Wednesday at ten o'clock in the morning, because I do not wish to wake you. I am taking care of transportation and food, so don't worry about a thing. Maybe they'll feed me at the hospital! I trust your health will be improving soon. Please let me know what your room number is and let everyone know that I will be arriving. SEE YOU THEN! Woo-hoo!

Your NEW FRIEND,

Phil

**Day 300.** I heard back from "Ruth":

Dear Beloved Phil,

I am glad you have successfully booked for a flight plane, and to rest assurably that I will reform the doctor and nurses of your arousal. I am in room 101 on the upper. I want you to know that I am a very devotion Christian and do only the things directed by God. All I need absolute trust and honesty when this funds get to you that I will be used to accomplish the purpose for which. Please contact the bank below for release of funds today. Please do not disappoint me for it takes

to entrust so much money on you. I have already issued a
letter of authority to the bank regarding my appointment as
my beneficial and you have to keep 20% for your services for
you and your entire household as a little token from my the
heart bottom. Contact the finance farm below as they am
expect you hear. You have to prove them with every assistance
for that the funds to release you without delays. If you are
prompting to the bank instructions this process will be
completed and you will have within 48 hours.

Yours Truly,

Ruth

**Day 302.** My dog, Mojo, senses it's Sunday. Every other day of
the week, she claws at my pants leg, begging to leave when I do. But
she knows dogs aren't allowed at church, so today she just hops onto
the back of the sofa and stares at passing cars. How does she know
this? Is it our late wake-up time (9:30 a.m.), or the clothes I am wearing (khakis and collared shirt)?

Pastor Rod has been chugging through a series on the book of
Daniel, and today he upped the ante a little by mentioning the Rapture of the church. He referenced 1 Thessalonians 4:15–17, in which
Paul talks of the return of Jesus to gather his saints and whisk them
skyward. There is, of course, some disagreement among believers on
precisely what this will look like.

A few maintain that the event will follow seven years of the
Great Tribulation. Most hope that Christians will be plucked from
the earth before they experience any difficulty at all, hangnails in-
cluded. A tiny minority, like last-days resident-expert Ernest Winkler, believe that our clothes will go with us to heaven.

My mind began flinging some thoughts around:

How many in this church will go? I mean, really? Ed Leaver is eighty-five, carries on a door-to-door soul-winning ministry, and calls the music here "wonderful." He will blow the roof off this place. But let's be honest, there are some unlikely candidates, though I shouldn't name them—even in a book on honesty.

Will the trumpet blast give the Rapture away, allowing certain people to hang on to folks like Ed Leaver in hopes they can hitch a ride?

What about my dog? If we're out for a walk and I've got her on a leash, she'll be fine. But what if the Rapture happens while we're sitting in church? Who will take care of Mojo? If she's left behind, she'll be confused, scared, hungry, and lonely. She'll be convinced I've abandoned her.

After church, Ramona said, "That was a great sermon." I didn't lie. I said, "I'm sure it was. But I missed most of it on account of more mental gymnastics. What will we do with me?"

"Keep you," she said. Hardly a day goes by when I don't smile and think: *She married me. Thank you, Lord.*

**Day 303.** Prophecy enthusiast Ernest Winkler is still energized by yesterday's Rapture talk. He called to tell me that the president of the United States is the Antichrist, that a one world currency has already been created, and that computer chips will soon be spliced into our foreheads or the backs of our hands (we'll get to choose the bodily location). I rarely see him this excited when there isn't a potluck dinner.

I'm still troubled about what to do with the dog. The kids will be going up with us, but I see no evidence in Scripture for our pets being called to heaven. I decided to ask my Facebook friends what they think, and a Bible college president said: "Maybe the dog will go first, and you'll be left behind."

**Day 304.** Additional Facebook friends are weighing in on yesterday's Rapture question:

- "Now you've got me worried. I have two dogs, at least three cats that we know of, four birds, several fish (six, I think) that can't go too long without food. I am planning on getting horses and possibly chickens in the future. This is really troubling!"
- "We'll find out when we get there. In the meantime, you shouldn't worry. I'm sure when [the] people [who are] left behind figure out how many people are missing, they'll round up the animals."
- "Why won't the animals go? The book of Isaiah says that the lion will lie down with the lamb."
- "You make a good point. With 80 percent of the country's population gone, it will turn into a postapoca-lyptic wasteland except for a few outposts of civiliza-tion. The abandoned dogs will go wild and roam the countryside in packs, terrorizing the locals."

This is not helping me sleep. My dog weighs eight pounds. Be-lieve me, she will be terrorizing no one.

One Facebook friend said, "If you really believe in the Rapture, you will find a nonbeliever and arrange to have your pet taken care of." Hmm.

**Day 305.** Today I spoke to a large group of public-school teach-ers. I enjoy speaking in nonreligious settings, although I didn't know there would be several thousand in the audience. I started out telling them, "It's a little ironic to be asked to speak to you, because I was homeschooled"—there was an uncomfortable pause, during which I could almost hear someone sharpening a harpoon—"until the age of five, at which point my mother gave up on me and turned me over to our educational system." They seemed to like this, so I kept going. I told them stories about a teacher who told me I'd never amount to anything, and one who believed I could. When I finally got around to my last point, "Live so the preacher won't have to lie at your funeral," they stood up and clapped like I had scored a touchdown. I wish my dad had been there. I think he'd be proud.

At a smaller workshop of four or five hundred, someone asked a question I sometimes dread hearing: "What religion are you?" I considered telling them "I'm a Trekkie." I even thought of confessing that I'm a Christian, but then wondered how many would immediately think of Uncle Bud, the Christian who ruins family reunions. So I said, "I'm really not into religion. I've tried it and I keep messing up. I'm a follower of Jesus of Nazareth, and I don't always do that great of a job." They liked that too and even asked me to return next year and tell them more.

We had a book table set up at the back of the room. My wife mentioned that audience members were stealing books off the table.

"Pray they'll read them before they roll 'em up and smoke 'em," I said.

**Day 306.** It's been an eyeopener, this correspondence with "Ruth." Time for one final e-mail.

> Subject: Great News. Really!
>
> Dear Ruth,
>
> I've got great news! Really! Promise me you will read to the end of this message, okay? Out of curiosity I entered your name on the Internet, and it looks like you have offered other people the same deal you offered me, only they paid money and received nothing in return. (Don't stop reading! There's great news ahead! Better than $25 million, I promise!) You have been stealing and using God's name in vain. I think you are smart enough to know that having money in this life is not worth eternal judgment in the next one. So here's the great news: God's grace is for all of us sinners, no matter what we've done! I have told lies too. I am guilty. But would you like to get rich quick? Here's how. Repent of your sin.

Ask Jesus to forgive you. Then return the money you've stolen and turn your back on sin. Zacchaeus did this in the Bible, and Jesus told him "salvation has come to this house."[1] God promises that when we trust him, he will give us "an inheritance that can never perish, spoil or fade…kept in heaven for you."[2] Is that cool or what? It's even better than a refund on a plane ticket!

I am praying today that you will read this and find the joy I have. Let me know when you do.

Sincerely in Jesus,

Phil

E-mail has made carefrontation almost too easy.

**Day 307.** I'm nearly eleven months into my truth vow, and finally there is an unexpected epiphany.

Promises of a meteor shower had me on a midnight stroll, to gaze into the heavens and praise God for his handiwork. But before I got around to praising God, I ended up severely miffed as I regurgitated the wrongs of my unfriend. What would drive a person to do this? Worse, I wished damnation upon him. Not eternal damnation, but plenty of the earthly variety.

The farther I got from town, the darker it became. I could scarcely see my feet, but the sky was becoming brighter. A thought jumped up and bit me: in the light of God's glory, none of us measures up. I have hurt others as surely as my friend has hurt me. One of the toughest surprises of my life is that good, Christian, churchgoing people disappoint. And some of the disappointing people are good people who nod along with the sermon.

I am among them.

A tiny glimpse at the darkness of my heart changes everything. To truly forgive another person I must acknowledge the sin in myself, the ease with which I have committed it, and the capacity for great wrongs that—apart from grace—I would surely commit every thirty-four seconds.

How can I not forgive when I have been forgiven so much?

**Day 308.** No Pac-Man tonight. Instead, I read that C. S. Lewis prayed every night for people he was tempted to hate. Hitler. Stalin. Mussolini. It's too late to pray for those guys, but not for my friend. I've concluded that God died for my friend as much as he died for me, and without God's help I'd be exactly where my friend is. Quite liberating, really.

It's like each time I forgive him, I set him free. Or maybe I set *me* free.

**Day 309.** Someone told FG what I said to the schoolteachers at the convention, and he thinks I caved in. He feels I should have hit them over the head with my Bible.

"Listen," I told him. "Next year you come along, and I'll ask you to share."

"No, no," he said. "I panic when I get in front of people."

"Me too." He thought I was kidding, but I was telling the truth. Thirty-seven different things keep me on my knees. Public speaking is in the top three.

**Day 310.** Today I hit pay dirt with www.postrapturepetcare .com, which has Matthew 24:36 (NLT) as its opener: "No one knows the day or the hour when these things will happen, not even the angels in heaven or the Son himself. Only the Father knows."

Then this compelling sales pitch:

Do you wonder what is going to happen to your pets when Jesus descends from Heaven…? Will your pets be left behind with no-one to care for them?

Have no fear! We at Post Rapture Pet Care are confirmed atheists and as such will be part of the left behind when the time comes. Just because we are atheists doesn't mean we are not animal lovers. We adore all kinds of pets and would love to look after your pets after you are gone.

For a small donation of £69.99 pounds, we will make sure your pets are well fed and taken care of long after you and your family have been taken up.

We have representatives in the South East of England and also in the North East of Scotland so can accommodate for most areas of the country giving you peace of mind where ever you are.

This is not a joke. We feel very strongly about pet care and want to offer the best possible services to British pet owners.

I e-mailed them immediately:

Your site looks great. Loved the "peace of mind where ever you are." We have a dog that is ten, so who knows which will be first, her death or the Rapture. (I guess you don't know either!) We live across the pond, a little to the north and a whole lot west of you (depending on which way you travel), so I don't imagine £70 is enough to make sure you'll attend to her over here after the Rapture. Any recommendations?

**Day 311.** I received a reply from the pet Rapture rescue people. They recommend some comrades in America, a group of "dedicated animal lovers and atheists." Sure enough, I found these confirmed moral atheists "with no criminal background." Their "network of animal activists are committed to step in when you step up to Jesus."

What I love about these guys is that they're active in twenty-four states, and they're cheaper than the Brits. They'll save additional pets for only fifteen dollars each. Unfortunately, there is fine print. They are "not equipped to accommodate all species" and they limit their services to "dogs, cats, birds, rabbits, and small caged mammals." But they do offer rescue services for horses, camels, llamas, and donkeys in New Hampshire, Vermont, Idaho, and Montana, which is nothing to sneeze at.

I wrote back immediately, of course:

Dear atheist friends!

I'm intrigued by your offer. We're interested but have a couple of questions. My Maltese Shih Tzu dog is ten. Does the contract expire after she dies (assuming of course that the Rapture hasn't happened yet)? Does your lifetime guarantee last for the life of my pet or for whatever pet I have during my earthly life? You mention additional pets being $15 each. I'm trying to figure out if the goldfish are worth the extra $15. Would this amount apply to each fish, or would you consider doing sort of a group price for a bowl of them?

Thanks!

Phil

**Day 312.** Today I spoke to James, who almost has his doctorate and knows about world religions. He feels I'm onto something with the Rapture pet project. "If anyone is going to take care of your post-Rapture pet, it should be an atheist," he feels. But he has concerns. What if they convince themselves it is a mass alien abduction and forget about your pet entirely? You don't want Buddhists caring for your animals, as historically dogs and cats have been fair game for them. Hindus may be the most reliable. Hindus do not eat pets, believing they could be a reincarnated uncle or aunt.

I checked the Internet for "Hindu Pet Rapture," but found nothing. Too bad. They could make a killing.

**Day 313.** With the onset of dementia, my mom's tact filter is irreparably broken. "Your nose is crooked," she told me today, then slugged me in the arm. She is well into her eighty-fifth year and still packs a wallop.

A nurse who is thickening a little through the middle poked her head in the door. "I have the FAT nurse today," Mom hollered.

I ducked and winced.

At least Mom wasn't swearing like a sailor. I know a guy whose mother was the star church pianist for thirty years, but now she drops cuss-bombs while he sings old hymns to her.

As I hugged Mom good night, she pulled me close and whispered, "This growing old ain't for kids."

**Day 314.** Mostly my prayers are polite and sanitized, like the ones we were taught to pray as kids, with our hands folded. I feel one thing; then I tell God another. Like a kid who fibs to a parent about playing with matches, not knowing that his pants are on fire.

But sometimes I discard the germ-free version of Phil Callaway and tell God what I really think, as if this comes as a complete surprise to him: *What? You struggle with envy? Phil! How long has this been going on?*

All in all, this honesty thing has been good for me. I've been dumping on God a little more, and I think he likes it. I think he'd rather hear my sincere—though venomous—outburst than my polite, sanitized denial. My lies during prayer have yet to fool him even once.

And so when our friend Kathy, who has raised twins after losing a husband in a single-engine plane crash, e-mailed to tell us that the cancer has spread to her liver, that the next round of chemo will start in two weeks, and that she is walking around in a fog, I said, "No, Lord, you can't allow this! No way!" Then I typed out a sterilized yet honest version of my prayer on the computer:

Dear Lord, you parted the Red Sea, you can handle this. Please do. We need you so badly. You put us in these fragile bodies and asked us to glorify you in them, but it's so hard to do. Please allow Kathy to see your good hand on her right now. Please numb the hurt and give her that peace you talk about. You've promised to care for the widows, and if you can't do it, then we are lost. We need to see that you are for us. We have nowhere else to turn.

I sent it to Kathy, wondering if she'd be offended at my bluntness.

**Day 315.** The Post Rapture Pet Care people replied:

Hi Phil,

Yes, I can tell by your e-mail that you are genuinely interested. I sense a degree of enthusiasm that I could literally cut with a knife. Yep, when your dog croaks, the contract is still in effect. No refunds. So unless you predict the Rapture happening over, oh say…the next three years, you'll likely be paying Rapture insurance for a dog corpse. We have no lifetime guarantee. We cover your pet rescue contract for ten years. I recommend you flush those fish down the toilet now and save the money. If you appreciate this site, you will enjoy my book. It's been receiving rave reviews on Amazon.

Yours in reason,…

**Day 316.** Ramona stuffs our tithe to the church in an envelope once a month and drops it in the offering. I've never liked this method. That leaves three Sundays a month when the ushers and fellow parishioners can see that we are putting nothing in the plate. So today I considered licking an empty envelope and dropping it in. I wonder if anyone else in all of church history has been hypocritical enough to think of doing such a thing.

Maybe I should put FG's name on it.

**Day 317.** I spoke at a strip club tonight. At least it once was, then some guys who love Jesus bought this old hotel, gutted the place, and restored it like new. God does well in the renovation business. Redeeming the wretched; making old things new. A hundred and twenty-five former addicts bunk here, learning life and career skills, studying the Bible, discovering how to get back into society as productive citizens.

One stood in front of us at this fund-raiser, a microphone in his hand. "I wandered around this city looking for a bridge that was high enough to jump off," he said. "But we're on the prairies. I couldn't find one. I've been in and out of jail I don't know how many times. I've been hooked on crack, sleeping on the street, left for dead. I wouldn't be alive without my friend." He can't talk for a minute and no one minds. Finally he managed to say, "My friend is Jesus."

I was supposed to make people laugh after this, but here I was wrestling tears.

"Every family has a secret," I told the audience. "It's something we're not eager to see on the evening news. My secret lives on Canada's worst street—East Hastings in Vancouver. We've tried to rescue David; he insists on living there. We've tried to visit him; he's hard to find. Surrounded by pimps and pushers and prostitutes, he collects cans and bottles. And he washes dishes in a hotel to support his habits. Diagnosed as schizophrenic, he has spent a lifetime being ridiculed, beaten, and bullied.

"He's my oldest brother."

I told them that I come from a long line of married people, but I also come from a long line of addicts. You name it, it liked us. A friend has said, "Never wrestle with a pig. You seldom win, and the pig kind of likes it." It's that way with addictions.

I told them the story of a father and son in Spain who fought

bitterly until the son left home to hit the streets. Wanting to recon-
cile, his dad took out an ad in a newspaper: "Paco meet me at the
Hotel Montana noon Tuesday all is forgiven papa."

Trouble was, Paco was a rather common name in Spain. At
noon on Tuesday, eight hundred men had gathered in the square. All
of them longing to be forgiven.[3]

"Beyond a shadow of a doubt, I would be on the street with
prodigal David, addicted to whatever I could beg or steal, were it not
for that forgiveness," I told them. And it's so true.

I tried to stop at that point, but I had to add one last thing. "I'm
the guy David the shepherd boy was talking about in the Psalms:
'Who can be compared with the LORD our God, who is enthroned
on high? He stoops to look down on heaven and on earth. He lifts
the poor from the dust and the needy from the garbage dump. He
sets them among princes, even the princes of his own people!'[4]

"The Bible tells us that we will all stand before God one day.
And we won't be asked what denomination we're from or what our
stand was on premillennialism. No, he will ask us if we fed the hungry, gave water to the thirsty, invited in strangers, clothed the naked,
cared for the sick, and visited the prisoners.

"So give to help this dream center. Just drop your Visa card in
the offering plate."

I believe a few of them did.

"I could have been on stage instead of you," one guy told me.
"I'm a professional whistler. I have a business card and everything."

"How long you been clean?"

"Nine months."

We did a high-five and hugged. We're just two guys who know
we can't breathe without grace.

**Day 318.** Busy day, but I found time to e-mail the Rapture pet
rescuer.

Ah, you think I jest? Well, I do. I heard what you're up to, and thought you and I would have a bit of a blast over a drink talking about it. How is it going for you? Seriously. Many bites? Congrats on your book. I've written a bunch myself. I'm interested in any stories about how it's going. I'm a follower of Jesus but not always a big fan of some of what I see in some of our churches. Christians are like manure, we do pretty well when we're spread out, but stink badly when you pile us together too long.

> All the best to you and yours!
> Phil

**Day 319.** Today I was seriously distracted by incoming e-mail:

Dear Phil,
> You mean you WEREN'T serious about needing our service? [He inserted a bad word here.] You came across so sincere. I have met so many really decent Christians as a result of this Web site that I'm actually amazed. Most of my interactions in debate rooms and message groups are with the complete [another bad word]. As a result my perspective of Christians has been influenced by the worst of them. It's comforting to realize that there are more like you than there are like them. I'll check out your writing, hopefully it's nonfiction. If you're ever in New Hampshire, give me a heads up. We'll do lobster.
> Best regards,…

**Day 320.** My daughter, Rachael, came with me to visit Mom at the nursing home. She leaned on Grandma's shoulder and sang in a sweet and quiet voice, "O God, our help in ages past, our hope for years to come..."[5] Grandma couldn't stop the tears and Rachael joined her.

I brought the dog along too. Mojo was the only one with dry eyes tonight.

**Day 321.** I called my scholar friend James, the PhD candidate, and read him the most recent e-mail from the Post Rapture Pet Care guy.

"You'll write him back, won't you?"

Of course I will. I really tried to think of something profound. Instead, I wrote this:

> You may have seen the bumper sticker "Jesus, deliver me from your followers!" That about says it for you, methinks. I'm sorry about the junk you've endured. I was raised by a little old mother who accepted and loved people, so that was always normal for me. She is battling dementia right now, but an atheist/agnostic/Buddhist friend wrote me to say, "Your mother was about the only Christian I could stand to be around." I'm sad if that's the case. Anyhow, I may have been insincere with my first note, but I do sincerely wish you all the best.
>
> > Your new friend (I hope),
> > Phil

I got an immediate response:

> Phil,
>
> > So sorry to hear about your mom's dementia. She sounds like a wonderful woman. She obviously did a good job with you. All my best to you as well. And don't forget, my invitation is always open.
> >
> > > Regards,...

I probably should have quit while I was ahead, but couldn't stop writing:

> For an atheist, you're incredibly kind. Hey…I'd be glad to
> send you a book. Just let me know your address, and I'll send
> you the book *Laughing Matters*. Hopefully, it won't be too
> preachy. It's a look at where to go when life stinks. Once I
> have your address, I'll send you monthly fund-raising mail,
> and six or seven door-to-door evangelists a week!
> Praying for you,
> Phil

**Day 322.** Today the man from Post Rapture Pet Care sent me his address, mailed me an atheist book, and commented on his new-found prayer support:

> Phil,
> So, praying for me, eh? Okay, that's fine. If you insist on
> doing that, then I will THINK for you.
> Yours in Reason,…

I hit Reply:

> Thanks so much! Believe me, there are days I could use you
> to do some thinking for me. I hope you have a great weekend.
> All the best,
> Phil

**Day 323.** Horrible cold coming on. Symptoms include sneezing, wheezing, whistling through my nostrils when I breathe, and the distinct feeling that an aardvark has crawled down my throat and is rooting around looking for snacks.

I said to Ramona, "Give me drugs."

She found some and said they're legal.

The side effects set in on the way to church. I sat in a pew undergoing mild hallucinations. Music was wonderful. Sermon was timely, timeless, and a bit brief. I loved everyone. I was even willing to overlook minor doctrinal differences. I felt particularly generous when the offering plate came by. No one shook my hand too hard as we were leaving. What a great church!

**Day 324.** Got a note from Kathy:

Thank you for your kind prayer. It brought tears to my eyes. It means so much to have friends who care and pray. I feel loved!

I replied with this.

You are loved so very much, Kathy. You've been one of those who has been living proof of the joy Jesus can bring in the midst of difficulty, but also one who's shown me to smarten up and be real! If we can do anything for you, please let us know.

Then I started hoping she wouldn't ask for much else. I'm really busy, you know, with this new ministry to atheists and all.

I felt immediate guilt and called Kathy to say that we'd be in her city in a few days and would love to see her. Unless she told us she wasn't available. "What can we bring?" I asked.

She said she'd love to see us. The chemo was postponed, so come by. But please don't bring anything.

"What about food?" I asked.

"Well, an odd thing is happening. The chemo has altered my tastes. The only things that taste good are sweets."

"My wife says that all the time. It's why she married me."

"But it's true. I've avoided sugar for years for health reasons. Anyway, there's not much on my diet list these days! What's sugar gonna do? Kill me?"

"What kind of sweet stuff do you like?" I asked. "You name it, we bring it. Seriously. Anything for you, kiddo. Just send me a list by e-mail."

**Day 325.** From Kathy:

This is almost too much! I feel like a kid in a candy store! It's hard to pick as I've avoided sugar for so long. Maple iced donuts, chocolate donuts, cherry strudel, ice cream bars. I can't think of anything else. I really shouldn't be eating any of this stuff, but right now there is not much I can handle eating! Looking forward to seeing you.

**Day 326.** Mom has been tired of this earth ever since Dad left it almost four years ago. She tries to make herself useful—pushes herself around her room cleaning everything twice, reads her large-print Bible with a magnifying glass, scribbles notes of encouragement to old friends. But the room is small and her eyes are dim and the notes are mostly illegible. A self-schooled grand-piano player, she sometimes coaxes notes from an old pump organ down the hall, but arthritis has crippled her fingers, and she can scarcely hear what she's playing anyway.

When I was a kid, she rubbed away the growing pains in my feet and legs. Tonight I'm returning the favor. I don't know if they have a medical term for her ailment. Shrinking pains, I suppose.

**Day 327.** We arrived at Kathy's house bearing sweets and plenty of strawberries, mangoes, kiwi, grapes, pears, and pomegranates. My wife insisted that Kathy eat "the sweet junk" with one hand while eating fruit with the other.

"This balances everything out," I told Kathy. "Remember Miss Piggy's Law of Eating: Never eat what you cannot lift."

Her doctor has told her to eat what she can, that her body will pull some good out of it, so she does. Ice cream bars, éclairs, cherry strudel, and a fruit buffet.

"One hundred percent natural," I told her. "No calories whatsoever."

She hasn't the energy to lift her grandson, but today her smile was contagious.

How do people live without the hope of eternity? How do they die?

## Honest Confession #11

I am a Christian because of God's grace. I find it in no other faith system. The Christian gospel is rather simple. I love the way Tim Keller puts it: "I am so flawed that Jesus had to die for me, yet I am so loved and valued and that Jesus was glad to die for me."[6] The result is that I neither swagger nor snivel; I live with thanksgiving, overwhelmed and overjoyed by grace. This path seems to lead us to a place of needing to be noticed less often, and being less concerned with how we're thought of.

# TWELVE

# Insomnia, Mormons, and More Angels

A lie has speed, but truth has endurance.

—EDGAR J. MOHN

**D**ay 328. I e-mailed the guy at Post Rapture Pet Care:

> If you were walking down a dark alley late at night all alone, and three buff and menacing guys were lumbering your way, would it make a difference if you knew they were coming from a Bible study?

**Day 330.** I haven't been sleeping well and the head cold hasn't helped. FG can tell. In the church foyer, he immediately diagnosed it as a spiritual problem and bid me trust God so that I could sleep like a log. "He giveth his beloved sleep," FG reminded me. I thought of smiting him, but refrained.

I decided to ask Andy (a childhood friend who sometimes poses deep questions) what he thinks. Andy is an agnostic. "Stop praying and see a doctor for sleep disorder," he insisted. "Prayer has shown no efficacy, medical science has."

I decide to do an experiment and see who's right. I will start with the agnostic's advice first.

**Day 331.** Last night when I couldn't sleep, I resisted the urge to take my requests to God and decided to watch the History Channel to see if that would help. I watched a special on life after people become extinct, where thousands of domesticated pets break loose and a deadly virus spreads. Thought, *We are all going to die off, so I might as well get some sleep.*

But I couldn't.

I turned the light on to read the Bible. Ramona woke up, witnessed this, and said, "On the way there, we should—" Then woke up again and said, "What's wrong? Are you okay?"

"Why?" I asked.

"You're reading the Bible."

Switched the light off and lay awake troubled by her words. My wife needs to see me reading the Bible more. I will do better, but I'll make sure the change is not too rapid or she'll think I'm doing it to impress her.

I wonder if I'd sleep better believing there is no God. My e-mail friend asserts that atheists have a better life because it's all they have. I disagree. Those who truly believe in heaven are of much earthly good.

Lying awake thinking about this didn't help me. Too bad there was no soccer match on TV. Unlike many of my friends, I find soccer a great sedative.

**Day 332.** I mentioned to my agnostic friend Andy that I would go see a doctor, but I don't want to depend on pills to sleep. He said it's a great idea to avoid chemical dependency and that what I need is a hot toddy. I once heard my grandpa speak of them with great fondness (hot toddies, not agnostics). Andy says that along about 9 p.m., I should follow these instructions:

Take the largest mug you can find and coat the bottom with honey. Squeeze ¼ of a lemon onto the honey. Pour an ounce of rum on top. Take a nip or two of rum for flavor. Heat water while sampling more rum. Find a tea bag, something caffeine-free (though it probably won't matter much at this point), repeat nips, and add the tea bag to make hot tea. Pour steaming tea into the mug and stir.

"Drink four of thozse, and you'll beep like a schlaby," he said. Funny guy, Andy. I kind of like him.

I couldn't find rum, but substituted cough syrup and slept like a baby—waking and screaming often.

**Day 333.** The Post Rapture Pet Care rep e-mailed again but evaded my question by asking one of his own:

If you needed to leave your six-year-old with a priest, youth pastor, or the town's auto mechanic for a few hours, who would you pick?

I tell him that much of what we see depends on what we're looking for, that I know and trust all three in our town, that we sometimes have lunch together. It's true.

I once thought that grace-killers and joy-suckers only resided in churches. Not so. Most of my correspondence with my new atheist friend over the last few days has turned to nonarguments and non sequiturs. I feel like I'm back on the playground and some guy is standing on the sidelines, yelling names at everyone but refusing to play.

I tell him that I don't want a fight—I just want him to consider for a moment the bizarre thought that I am not completely insane and have reason behind my faith. If I'm wrong, I've lived a life filled with joy and struggle and peace and hope. If he's wrong, then what?

"Please don't have on your tombstone: 'All dressed up, no place to go,'" I write.

But it's not working.

Guess I'll just pray for him. It has come to this.

**Day 334.** Why can't I sleep? Sleep was God's idea, so was medication. He gave the first sleeping pill to Adam so he could remove one of his ribs and create a woman, of whom Adam said in Hebrew, "Wahoo!" God formed horses able to sleep standing up (humans too—I've seen it). He created snails that will hibernate up to three years, for Pete's sake. The brown bat spends twenty hours a day zonked out, the African elephant only 3.3 hours, and the giraffe less than two. A human baby is dead to the world sixteen hours a day (the other eight are when his parents are trying to sleep), and I need at least seven hours to remain productive and relatively noncranky.

"Please, Lord, give me sleep. There are agnostics and atheists out there sleeping soundly. Knock me out so I can serve you better tomorrow."

**Day 335.** I lay awake for three hours telling God that I trust him entirely, praying for my e-mail atheist friend, wishing I could tell my readers of his conversion. Wouldn't they be impressed?

I quoted verses about peace that my mother drummed into me years ago. About two thirty, I turned on the TV and found a soccer match.

Out like a light.

**Day 337.** FG could tell by the rings under my eyes that he needs to offer more sleep advice. This time he seemed open to the possibility that it may be something other than a spiritual problem. Yes, it may be a result of a culture that has begun to despise sleep. Seventy million Americans have sleep disorders, he said. Back in 1850, when our great grandparents lugged coal for a living, they slept nine and a half hours per night. But now, with electric lights, cable TV, the Internet, and alarm clocks, we are down to seven hours.

Then he asked: "Have you been putting my name on blank offering envelopes?"

I interrupted him: "Did you know that nine months after the New York ice storm of 1998 there was a baby boom?"

FG didn't know this and walked away puzzled.

**Day 338.** 5:35 a.m. Why did I set two alarm clocks again? Oh yes, so I wouldn't miss my flight. I have an impeccable record when it comes to not missing flights. I'm scheduled to speak to a convention that attracts a large number of funeral-home people. They see enough sorrow and death, so I'll talk about life and hope. Better get up.

5:44 a.m. Can't believe it. Snow. Snow? In May? Six inches of stupid snow. I wonder if the same people who forecast our weather are the ones who are so sure of global warming?

5:58 a.m. I shake wet snow from a severely burdened tree in the front yard. Unfortunately, my arms are only about three feet long, so shaking the trunk has every layer of me covered. I brush snow off the car and I'm off, dripping wet and shivering. Two hours until the flight leaves. One hour to the airport. Shouldn't be a problem. The car heater should start working just before I arrive.

6:37 a.m. The roads are horrible, so I'm crawling along. My car hydroplanes and I enter the lane reserved for oncoming traffic, narrowly avoiding someone's headlights. I try to ease the wheel to the right. No sir. I plunge into a ditch, scattering stupid snow and stupid slush and whatever other kinds of white crud fell out of the sky last night. Car's up to the frame in slush and ice. "Help, Lord!"

6:38 a.m. Angel One arrives. He drives a white pickup truck. He also smokes a cigar and is swearing like it's his native tongue. Probably a backslidden angel. "Where the blank you going?" he asks. "Get your blank in here, I'll drive you." I tell him I'm going to the airport, but there's no way I'll make my eight o'clock flight.

"Don't give up yet." He takes a long pull on the cigar. "I'll drive you part way."

You don't argue with angels.

6:40 a.m. I tell Angel One that I am meeting someone at the airport and dial Gord's cell phone. "Just hit the ditch," I tell him. Gord thinks I'm joking. "Yaright!" He laughs, and *click,* he hangs up. Make mental note not to joke so much on the phone.

7:11 a.m. "This is as blanking far as I go," says Angel One, skidding to a stop on the outskirts of town. "I'll just find someone going to the blanking airport." I leave one of my books on the front seat, along with a thank-you note, as the angel flags down the first car. "I'll take him," hollers Angel Two, who drives a white Chrysler.

On a clear day, the airport is only forty-five minutes from this spot. My flight departs in forty-nine minutes. I won't be speaking to the funeral-home people today. I don't have enough faith to even pray about it. But I tell Angel Two all about it.

"Not to worry." He smiles. "I work at the airport. We'll get there."

7:13 a.m. I call Gord again. This time he doesn't hang up. "There's no way I'll make it," I tell him. "I'm forty-five minutes out."

"Don't give up," he says. "Tell the guy if he gets you here, I'll give him NHL tickets or cash. His choice."

7:22 a.m. Gord calls me.

"Doesn't look good. No more flights leave here today after this one. How far out are you?"

"Forty minutes."

Gord groans. "I'll get my wife to pray," he says. I know Liz. She has a direct line.

"I work for a charter airline," says Angel Two.

"How much to get me there?" I ask.

"Three thousand bucks." Must be a Baptist angel.

7:50 a.m. It's Gord again. "Don't give up," he says. "They're holding the plane." This does not happen outside the movies, but it's happening for us. "He's two minutes away," I hear Gord mention to someone at check-in. *Impossible,* I'm thinking. *Can't happen.*

7:53 a.m. Security is taking swabs of my laptop. It's a good thing I didn't bring my lap dog.

7:59 a.m. "Welcome aboard," says a flight attendant, grinning at Gord and me. "We're set for an on-time departure."

We're settled in our seats and Gord admits, "I sort of lied to the airline. Told them you were speaking at a funeral home."

"I am," I say.

"Everything changed when I told them that."

"Did you say someone had died?"

"No."

"Then we're okay, aren't we?"

"I dunno, you're the guy who's writing about lying."

**Day 339.** Yesterday Gord and I made our flight by barely a whisker. I know not how. Folks who travel a lot, like I do, know that you can't count on miracles, so we plan ahead, watch weather forecasts, and leave early. Perhaps God wanted me to talk to the funeral-home people.

I arrived in the right city and got to the funeral-home-directors convention. I had barely dried out when I told them they had chosen their occupation wisely. One hundred percent of people are now dying, so job security is high in their line of work. I told them how to really live while they're surrounded by death. And my last point was this: courage is fear that has said its prayers. I didn't have to look far for illustrations. I told them about my day of near misses and that I really didn't think a storm and a ditch and an airline schedule are that big a deal for God, so maybe whatever is troubling us today is manageable when we trust a God this big. They liked the thought of that.

Back home, a friend picked me up at the airport. I called Gord to thank him for a memorable day. While I was on the phone, I couldn't help saying, "Help! We hit the ditch!"

That's when the phone went dead.

**Day 340.** I finally got desperate enough to see a doctor. He asked if I was on any medications, and I told him about the stuff my wife was giving me. He said, "Whoa! A bear couldn't sleep taking that stuff!"

He prescribed some cold medication. I went home and slept almost nine hours.

**Day 341.** My healing could not have been more timely. I'll be speaking at a mayor's prayer breakfast tomorrow. My friend James is going with me for companionship. And laughs. And to keep me in line. I'm too weak to travel alone, and it's surprising how many friends you have when you buy them meals.

After a massive dinner, we waddled through the seedy side of town to our posh hotel.

"I need some help." It was a guy my age, missing a few teeth, with a wool hat pulled down to his bushy eyebrows.

"What would you like?" I asked.

"I'm hungry."

"Where would you eat if you could?"

"There's a diner around the corner." He pointed in that direction.

We sat at a wobbly table, the three of us, and Eddie rattled on with his story. An abusive dad. On the streets at age twelve. He sleeps in a red tent in a grove of trees near our hotel.

Bruises and sores covered Eddie's needled arms. "AIDS," he said. "Can you buy me some smokes?"

"I'm not old enough to buy smokes," I told him. He grinned. "But I'm happy to buy you food." Eddie munched in tiny bites and stuffed most of his dinner into a gnarled backpack.

"You ever heard of Jesus?" I asked him.

Eddie's grin grew wider. "Yep."

"If he were here, he'd tell you how much he loves you and he'd heal you. Give you the hope of heaven. Do you have that?"

"Yep."

James bought him a breakfast ticket, and we strolled the street together, Eddie puffing out his chest when his friends looked our way.

"Will I see you there?" I asked, pointing skyward.

"Yep." He gave us a three-tooth smile, and we were on our way.

**Day 342.** Seven hundred of the business elite attended the breakfast this morning. Even while I was speaking, I couldn't stop thinking about Eddie. I wish I'd found a way to sneak him in there.

I don't know why I was born in white suburbia and had a backyard full of friends who didn't snort cocaine or use needles. I don't know why my parents stuck around, put me through school, tucked me in, and said, "I love you."

I don't know why I was born in a small town where nobody shoots anyone and they cash my checks without asking for ID. But I do know that looking at Eddie with anything less than compassion is arrogant and wrong and foolish.

Tonight, more than ever, I'm wanting to extend grace to others. And I'm longing for a time when God will make all things new and right.

**Day 343.** Two guys in white shirts and dark ties came up the walk when I was about to wash my car. I wasn't pushing a lawn mower or wearing earphones, still it was déjà vu from a scene I imagined just a few months ago. They asked if I'd read their blue book. I told them I had. (And I didn't resort to sign language.)

"What did you think?" asked one. "Did you pray? Did you sense a special revelation?"

"Yes, I prayed. No, I didn't sense anything special. But can I tell you something? My mother is not long for this world. When I visit her at night, she wants me to read from a book beside her bed that's almost worn out. It's the Bible. It changed her life when she was a teenager. It has changed mine too."

I continued: "You know, there are twenty-five thousand biblical sites that have been confirmed by archaeological discoveries, but your book doesn't have even one?" I've rarely used bigger words.

"But people have died for this book," one of the guys said.

"People have died for the Koran," I mentioned. "Does that make it true?"

"Well," the other guy stammered, "we're not here to argue. You're smarter than us."

Never in my life had anyone ever said that to me. I had to laugh.

"No, I'm not smarter," I admitted. "I'm just forgiven. Covered in God's grace. I hope you'll spend your lives learning to love Jesus Christ."

"Uh...is there someone else we can talk to in this town?"

I grinned. "You want me to do a referral?" How crazy do they think I am? Then I had an idea. "Tell you what. If you go up this street and take a right, then go four blocks, you'll find a little white house on the left. Picket fence. Great guy. His initials are on his mailbox. FG."

**Day 344.** I filled out a visitor's card at church and slid it into the offering plate after my wife put in a check with one too many zeros on it.

Under the section "What can we do for you?" I wrote, "I have very little time to cut my grass this week. Could someone do that for me? I would be happier than I have ever been if that were to happen!"

"What did you write?" Ramona whispered.

I couldn't help snickering. Everything's funnier when it's not supposed to be.

**Day 345.** So far this honesty thing has cost me very little. But today that changed. A company promised to hack the cost of my car insurance in two, so I spent an hour on the phone with an insurance agent. With the information almost computed, she asked, "Will you be using the car for transportation of commercial goods?"

I paused.

"Yes," I told her, but a small amount of goods, not really anything substantial, just wee little insignificant things like books.

"Would these books fit into a briefcase?"

I paused again.

"How…um…big a briefcase are we talking about? I'll bet they make some big ones now."

She wasn't buying it. "How many pounds would they weigh?"

I said I didn't really know, but that they weren't that heavy. I can carry them around.

"A little box?" she asked, patiently.

"Um, no. A few boxes."

"How many times a year do you speak?"

"More than a few." She waited for me to come clean. "Quite a… More than a few."

I am denied insurance on account of them not insuring business vehicles. My truth vow has now cost me:

- $5.00 root beer payback from 1981 (long before accepting the truth assignment)
- $45.00 on dinner and golf (Day 10)
- $55.00 that Ramona refused to accept from a waitress (Day 56)
- $0.49 (Day 61)
- $1,500.00 per year on vehicle insurance (today)
- Total: $1,605.49. Not that I'm counting.

Is there some way this might earn me eternal rewards? If my mother was right in saying that virtue is its own reward, when will I see some of it?

**Day 346.** I was thinking of fabricating a great story today. Something about leading my atheist friend at Post Rapture Pet Care to Jesus. Wouldn't that be a blessing and a big encouragement to readers? I've never done this, but others have. It's strange and a little frightening that it would even cross my mind.

**Day 347.** Mom's speech is down to a few faint murmurs, nothing discernible, but I keep my head up, smile widely, and talk lots. I'm discovering that I can talk for almost an hour without saying much, and I agree with myself most of the time.

Mom's eyes are glazed over, and I utter words I had never thought to say before. "It's okay, Mom. You can go home now. We'll miss you here, but it's okay."

Later on, sitting in the car, I unloaded my frustrations on God: "Why do saints who served you so well end life like this? When she's staring at the wall looking troubled, are you there with her? Is she all right?"

Some remnant of an old pop song played through my mind. About treasuring the questions when we run out of answers. How one day we will know.

"God, I haven't asked you for much lately, but would you take Mom soon? She wants to see Dad. And would you take her in her sleep? I'd like that. Thanks."

**Day 348.** No one showed up to cut my grass. Is there a secretarial strike? What if I went and cut the church secretary's grass? But then what if people were to think I was flirting with her?

I decided to renew the vitality of my marriage by renting the movie *Jaws*. Ramona and I watched it today with our feet in a large bowl of water. I've come a long way in the fear department since I first watched this movie back in ninth grade, after which I did not take a bath for six months.

**Day 349.** Tonight as I tried to feed Mom ground beef and mashed veggies, she stubbornly refused. Clamped her mouth shut and turned her head to the wall. I tried the same things that she tried on me when I was little, in an attempt to trick me into eating mashed goulash.

"Open up the hangar, here comes the plane."

She clenched her lips and closed her eyes.

"Open up the tunnel, here comes the choo-choo."

She made loud raspberry noises.

I wonder if she was dreaming of a grander feast in another land.

When your mama has caught dementia, there's comfort in knowing that it's not who you remember but who remembers you.

**Day 351.** Family members arrived one by one to be with Mom at the nursing home. My siblings are a zany lot, and people poked their heads into the room marked "Respite" to see why we were laughing. We have church here in the hospital, singing hymns and the songs Mom loved when she was a girl. Most of the words we couldn't remember, but she appreciated the effort. We tried to carry on with some semblance of normalcy, but there is nothing normal about taking turns sleeping in a hospital, waking up to listen for raspy breathing.

**Day 352.** Not a day has passed when I haven't thought about my atheist e-mail pen pal. The correspondence is now on again and I'm enjoying it. Confiding about my mother has brought out his compassionate side.

I'm considering a new and honest course. What if I were to get to know him and hear him, not as a project or some potential notch in my gun, not in an "I'm right/you're wrong" way, but as a guy Jesus loves?

Yes, he's angry, but he's thoughtful, intelligent, and from time to time, funny too. Maybe one day he'll take a truth vow himself. One wherein he has the integrity to admit that God's nonexistence can't be proven scientifically, nor can his existence. Truth, after all, is not a politician who changes policies to get reelected. It's what it is, like it or lump it.[1]

My atheist friend's eternal destiny is not my responsibility. Loving him is. From now on, I'll try all bait, no switch.

**Day 353.** Mom is fading fast. The nurse asked me for "the family's wishes." We can keep her alive awhile, she said.

"Her wish was that when this old body gives out, she'd go home to heaven," I said, smiling. "I'd like her to be as comfortable as possible. And we kids will be here with her."

The nurse smiled. "I'm so relieved. You're making the right decision, you know. We can hook her up to some tubes. I've seen them hang on for months."

I told her of Mom and Dad's sixty-two-year marriage. Of Dad's comb-over, of the laughter in our home, of these two dear saints and their love for Jesus.

When the nurse said good night, I sat by Mom's bed, warming her hands and thanking her for such great memories. I don't think she could hear me, but you never know. I'd like to have said these things more often, years ago.

**Day 354.** An unexpected letter arrived from my homeless brother, David. It was addressed to Mom Callaway. In fifty years he has written only a handful of letters home. This is the first since Reagan was president. My brother Dan read it aloud to Mom. David told her what a great and godly mother she has been, how he loves her. He said he wants her to take good care of herself and "thanks for everything."

Though she was clearly in pain, her chest rising to catch the next breath, still she found the strength to nod her head. Somehow a smile spread across her face, like a welcome anesthetic.

**Day 356.** It's strange to find comfort in a dog. But there is one sitting on my lap, head cocked, looking at me as if I'm the center of the known universe. The kids have taught this animal to sit, beg, jump, turn around, roll over, lie down, shake with the wrong paw, and play dead. Now the dog is teaching me a few tricks.

Tonight, as if I don't have enough troubles, I pick up the newspaper. There's unrest in the Middle East, and pirates are commandeering ships off the coast of Somalia. I see more murders mentioned than you'd find in a Coen brothers movie.

Mojo noses the paper aside and wants my attention. I'm thinking, *I wonder if this pathological dictator is really gonna launch nuclear warheads,* and my dog is thinking, *I wonder if he's gonna give me a lick of that ice-cream cone.*

One of us is thinking, *How can these things possibly work out for good?* The other is thinking, *I sure wish he'd put down the paper and open up a can of tuna.*

I suppose a good dog knows that newspapers are useful for certain things, but it also knows that worry is like a rocking chair. It gives you something to do, but doesn't take you anywhere.

**Day 358.** 10 a.m. My wife and kids and I headed to the lake while many of our friends were in church. Tom took us across the water with his V8 inboard like we are trolling for fast-moving trout. I reminded myself that Abraham didn't go to church, and I kept the cell phone ready for news of Mom.

Later, back on land, we parked around a campfire, and after eating hot dogs, we played Pass the Shoe. It was new to me too. Someone tells about what God's doing in his or her life, then tosses a shoe at whoever has the most fear in his or her eyes. They share next, and on it goes. We were joined by others.

Emma asked why she couldn't be baptized that day in the lake. Chloe suggested that Emma should wait to be baptized in front of her church body as a witness, but couldn't think of a scripture to back up that idea.

I thought, *I'll tell you why she shouldn't be baptized. People on the beach will think we're nuts, that's why.* But like Chloe, I failed to think of a scripture to hide behind.

A few others shared about hard lessons God had taught them, then Emma said, with tears splattering her cheeks: "But I want to be baptized."

Everyone looked at me as if I were a priest and had enough clout with God to do it. Someone had a Bible, so I read the story about the Ethiopian eunuch and Philip, and how the eunuch asked the same question Emma was asking. I was hoping there might be something in the story that would provide a loophole. After Philip baptized the eunuch, the account says, "The Spirit of the Lord suddenly took Philip away."[2] I made a little joke about it.

I asked Emma if she is a for-sure born-again Bible-believing, Jesus-following, accountable-to-her-community Christian. She said yes, she loves Jesus, but that she's weak in her faith.

I said, "Welcome aboard."

A dozen of her friends and family gathered on the beach, along with curious onlookers. I baptized her in the name of the Father, the Son, and the Holy Spirit.

I forgot to plug her nose, and she took on some water, but when she could breathe again, she couldn't stop thanking me and hugging her fiancé. Her eyes glowed like those rechargeable yard lights that can't stop shining because they've been staring at the sun all day.

9:00 p.m. Tomorrow is my sister, Ruth's, birthday. We visited Mom together, and Ruth told me she's been praying that God would take her on her birthday.

"God would take Mom or you?" I asked.

Ruth brushed tears aside, laughed, and slugged me. If Mom were alert, I bet she'd blame me for starting it.

## Honest Confession #12

Back when I was still a devout Pharisee, I scowled at those who talked about grace, assuming they wanted both salvation and permission to do whatever they pleased. And when I came to discover grace as a biblical concept, it frightened me at first. The old idea of being saved by works has its benefits. It's a system where God owes you. You've been helping him out with all your good deeds. He can't very well put you through difficulty, since you're a taxpayer. You've paid your dues, you have your rights. But the beyond-belief teaching of grace is that we get what we can never pay for and more, including joy and hope and the desire to please him. I like living by God's grace a lot better than relying on my own efforts.

# THIRTEEN

# Safe at Home

I live life without pretending. I'm a sucker for happy endings.

—CHRIS RICE

While it is well enough to leave footprints on the sands of time, it is even more important to make sure they point in a commendable direction.

—JAMES BRANCH CABELL

**D**ay 359. Some find it not entirely coincidental that my mother went to Glory this morning, at the exact time a power plant in our town went up in flames. Given my reputation for mischief, several have asked exactly where I was at 6 a.m. I was asleep in bed. I have a witness. My wife was sleeping too, when the phone rang.

Our daughter was with her cousin Lena, just a few feet from the grandest graduation ceremony a soul could wish for: the passing of her grandmother into the presence of Jesus.

I haven't been much good to anyone today. Mostly I've stood around thinking, *I'm an orphan now, be nice to me.* And people are.

Our church can't do enough, and there's an avalanche of food in the kitchen. We could set up a food kiosk to pay for the funeral.

I'm feeling several emotions all at once. Deep sorrow, of course. For the passing of an era. For having to say a final good-bye to my biggest fan. Strangely, I feel guilt for being thankful that she's gone, that there's no more dementia. I try to imagine her without it, slipping into heaven with a twinkle in her eye to see what Jesus has been building for her.

I bet the second person to greet her is Dad. I bet he says, "Pucker up, Bernice. Welcome home!"

**Day 360.** The nursing home called early to tell us Mom's stuff needed to be out of her room by noon, on account of someone else moving in. We would be charged for an extra day if we didn't hurry. Thoughts of respectfully asking the administrator to place the phone cord about his neck and pull upward played through my tired mind, but I couldn't bring myself to say it.

Someone has joked that death is not the end—there's the fighting over the will. Thankfully, there's not much to fight over.

We removed all of Mom's earthly possessions in four small grocery bags. They contained two George Beverley Shea CDs, a boom box, two bags of clothing, eyeglasses, her wedding ring, three teddy bears, a Bible, and some books—including one of mine with the corners curled up and smiley faces throughout.

I sat in the car and cried. Strangers walked by and I pretended to be fiddling with the CD player. Then I sat there and bawled for two solid minutes, something I hadn't done since my wife dumped me back in high school—when she was my girlfriend.

How do you say good-bye to the first woman who ever kissed you? The one who rocked you and read to you and showed you where to find Jesus? How do you say good-bye to one of the greatest apologetics for Christianity you ever met, the one who knelt with you by your Styrofoam bed when you were five to listen to you ask

Jesus to be your Savior and friend? Well, first you cry a lot. And then you smile, because you remember how imperfect she was.

Mom was shy on fashion sense, and she hated cooking. Her second-favorite kitchen activity was preparing dinner. Her favorite was banging her head against the fridge. She once tied me to the clothesline with a dog collar and leash. I quite enjoyed sitting on the back step pondering a dog's life. I had never seen the world quite this way. A dog doesn't have much to do, you know, just sit there and watch for movement. Mom felt so guilty she released me with a warning: "Stop running away." And I did. Mom would have been reported for such behavior nowadays, but mothers weren't perfect back then. They weren't absent either.

The same strangers came out of the nursing home, walking past my car and noticing me inside. But this time I was laughing. I held my hand to my ear like I was talking on a cell phone, though I had left mine at home.

8:45 p.m. Bud Marsh and his wife dropped by to comfort us in our grief. I almost wept when I saw them coming up the walk, Bud with an ample sized Bible in his hand and his wife with a hanky. I hadn't talked with them ever before, except for the time Bud thought I belonged to a different family and mistakenly witnessed to me when I was ten. I fled to my study hollering to Ramona the words of Adam from Genesis 3: "I was naked; so I hid."

Ramona didn't buy it. She said, "You've got clothes on, get out here."

Bud and his wife are not affiliated with any church, per se; they are "itinerant ministers." Mrs. Bud said she met my mom before I was born and just wanted to come by and weep with those who weep. She proceeded uninvited to our couch, where she sat down with a loud sigh and said, "Well, I guess God needed her more than you did." Then she sat there sniffling into her hanky. Bud nodded meekly and clutched the Bible. (His wife forms the speaking part of their team.) When she composed herself, she continued, "God never gives us more than we can handle. I know just how you feel, but time really does heal all wounds, you know? I remember the time—"

I was studying a souvenir my son Steve brought me from Ukraine, a heavy wooden mace with frighteningly sharp points on the business end. It was resting on a windowsill just inches from Mrs. Bud's head, and I was shocked at the little scenario that played out in my mind. It was most likely the result of my watching too many Alfred Hitchcock movies.

"God works all things together for good," said Mrs. Bud. Amazingly, there was no blood on her sweater; she had not been bludgeoned. "A few months and you'll be praising God for this, Bill, so try to look for the good in it."

"Gerald," her husband corrected her. "Where did you get Bill? It's Gerald."

Ramona was trying to mask a snicker.

"No problem," I said, standing and inching toward the door. I couldn't help thinking what a comfort it would be if they left.

**Day 361.** I received more e-mails and phone calls. "I never heard your mom gossip," wrote one. She's right. You were safe at our house. I never once heard Mom speak an unkind word about my papa, a preacher, or even a politician. She had such little discernment, it was frightening. She would defend complete idiots sometimes. Referees on Monday Night Football, for instance. I guess she figured God had shown so much grace to her, she'd better show some to others.

Mom suffered through the Great Depression, and through a not-so-great depression herself. In my earliest memories, she is sick in bed, unable to make meals for weeks. College girls would come to clean our house and to cook, and I liked that. But I think I got into comedy to cheer my mother up. I would make faces for her, do cartwheels, and whatever it took to make her smile. I hoped she'd laugh out loud, then get up and dance like she did sometimes—though our church forbade us from even trying it at home.

One summer vacation, I watched her hand gospel tracts to leather-clad bikers, telling them that Jesus was wild about them. I was sure they would murder her—and me—but they didn't. Her charm was irresistible, even to Hells Angels.

Mom was fearless, yet she was the first person I ever saw have a panic attack. From her I learned that our greatest saints often struggle the most. They grow saintly hanging on to Jesus with everything they've got.

Her funeral is tomorrow. Better find my sunglasses.

**Day 362.** We laid my mom to rest beneath the broad prairie sky. It seemed hardest for the grandkids. But I cried too. I remembered that time back in third grade when Mom had been gone on a trip to the city. All day I had suspected she'd died in a horrible car crash. So when the bell rang, I took off for home.

When our house came into view, she was standing on the back step on tiptoes, hanging clothes out to dry. I hid behind some lilac bushes, ashamed of myself and my worry, ashamed of all the tears. Our jet black dog, Inky, found me, and Mom asked if I was okay. I should have told her then that I adored her, that she was the best mom a kid could hope for. I should have told her I was the envy of the neighbor kids all because of her.

Can she know these things in heaven? Does she know that back on time-locked planet Earth, there's a grown-up kid who can't stop thanking God for her legacy? That I'm fully aware the lines have fallen to me in pleasant places, that I have a goodly heritage?

I told people at the funeral that our town lost a power generator this week and a great generator of power, all at once. Mom prayed almost nonstop as her years increased. Three best-selling authors said they wouldn't have written a paragraph without her encouragement. The same is true for me. Mom was a writer who was content to stay at home while her books traveled the world. She could have secretaried, administrated, or managed a staff, but she showed me that money is a lousy substitute for the adoration of five kids and thirteen grandchildren. And it was those children who stood around her bedside singing hymns through their tears, thanking God for her life.

My brother-in-law Lauren was smiling at me, knowing he'll likely see her before I do.

Decked out in a three-piece suit, our adopted son, Paul, came to pay his respects to a lady who loved him the way he was—cigarettes and all.

How do you say good-bye to such a girl? Maybe you don't. You say thank you. Thanks for the love and the inspiration and the memories. And thank you, Lord, that you took her in her sleep. And that because she's with you and you're with me, we aren't so very far apart.

Heaven is looking sweeter all the time.

**Day 363.** Losing someone you love, especially a parent, gives you good reason to look back over a lifetime. It's a chance to reflect on that person's life and on your own.

My parents' backyard was a place where my friends knew they could play football, baseball, and ball hockey without being yelled at or threatened with live ammunition. My mom chose to nurture children over growing grass. I received an e-mail from a boyhood friend who told me that Mom regularly hugged kids who had more tattoos than brain cells. Perhaps it was her bad eyesight, or perhaps she had very good eyesight—so good that she only saw the stuff that mattered.

Note to self: Be nicer to my kids' friends. Forget earrings, tattoos, and similar issues. Love them anyway. One day they might write a note about me to my kids.

**Day 364.** 4:30 a.m. On what would very likely be Mojo's last day on earth, she stood by my bed scratching at my arm, wanting to be let out. I squinted at the alarm clock and muttered, "Bad girl, go back to sleep."

My wife rolled over and said, "Huh?"

5:30 a.m. The dog wanted out again, and I hadn't been sleeping anyway, so I sat on the deck, grinning and watching the sun rise while Mojo engaged in highly important tree-to-tree activity.

This dog is not at all like the dogs of my childhood. Those were manly dogs. Our terrier, Inky, lived to surprise people. Folks who strolled by our house late at night, gazing upward and admiring the northern lights, had no idea how fast they could run until Inky showed them. I think Inky was put on earth to bring people closer to God. We would hear folks crying out to God as they sprinted past in the dark. They were so deeply impacted, they wrote letters to my parents.

Dad sold Inky to a glue factory and brought home Lady, an Irish setter that drooled like a bad tap. Lady helped me get ready for school each morning. She could wash my face in two seconds flat.

One Sunday we came home from church to discover that she had eaten the soles from our shoes. Or at least one from each pair. The preacher had spoken of patience and how tribulation helped it work, but I don't think Dad was listening. He gave Lady away that afternoon, and within a week she gave birth to twelve handsome puppies. I kid you not. I spent that summer asking for one. I also spent it barefoot. Except for Sunday mornings.

8:30 p.m. I was walking to the front of the house, dog beside me, when she spied a cat across the street and took off after it like she'd been shot out of a gun. I could hear a van coming down the street and was powerless to stop it. It was also too late for the driver to stop. She hit the brakes and the tires squealed. Too late.

I watched in horror as our dog skidded underneath the van. She actually ran under the front tire and shot out the back. Then she turned to me, let out a timid yip, and just sat there, dazed and grinning—this dog with nine lives, sitting there like a toddler that just survived a water slide.

10:30 p.m. I prayed, "Dear God, thanks for sparing my dog. I'm not sure how I would have handled things right now."

10:33 p.m. Ramona looked my way and said, "Good night, Gerald."

**Day 365.** Today I felt lightheaded and borderline happy to be at church. FG was the greeter, and he used both hands and a tight grip to welcome me.

"Crud," I said. "Go easy on the handshake. You're not riding a bull." I knew my hand would hurt until Thursday, but I forgave him.

"I'm sorry you lost your mom," he said.

"Thanks, but I didn't. I know exactly where she is."

It was the first time ever that I've corrected FG's doctrine, and it felt rather nice.

Milton, the church wit, didn't yet know about my mother. He had a joke—something about a health store being closed due to illness—and though it wasn't top drawer, I managed a laugh.

I even found myself looking forward to the sermon, thankful for the dear people around me, knowing that I wasn't at church to get something for Phil but to hear from God, to express my love for him.

Before the service, I prayed that God will BLESS my enemy friend. What has come over me? I'm beginning to genuinely want the best for him! Honest. I even found myself praying for his wife and child.

We stood to sing, all except for Kevin's eldest daughter, who was holding her invalid sister, rocking her slowly, while the whole family sang the words of Job, "You give and take away… Blessed be the name of the Lord."[1]

The song leader must have forgotten to tune his guitar between services, but who cares?

I found a note in my Bible that Kevin slipped me. It was an honest poem that he wrote to his baby girl.

Am I selfish to want you to stay with me,
    instead of going to be with Him?
To stay where I can shake your little hand
    or pat your chest
      and watch your crooked smile?

Am I selfish to want a little more time,
    to learn to love you more?
And not be angered by the way
    your life imposes on mine?

But if you go, you'll be home with Him,
    the One who made you
    and loves you best.
Each breath will be sweet and easy.
Running, jumping, smelling, seeing,
    learning, talking, loving…

I will let you go if you want to,
    but know that your daddy's selfish
    and wants you to stay![2]

I got so carried away, I lifted my hands along with Kevin. Thank you, Jesus, for amazing grace.

# Life After the Truth Experiment

Tonight I lounge on the back deck while the sun slips toward the distant mountains. Ramona arrives with drinks and says, "Whatcha doing?"

"Nothing."

She smiles. "You did that yesterday."

"I wasn't finished."

She massages my shoulders. "You're tense. Relax."

"Ya, a few things have been happening. Ahhh, just a little lower on the left."

The dog cocks her head to one side, crouches, then springs onto my lap, hoping I'll pay the massage forward.

"Let's take a vacation," says Ramona. "We can start tonight."

By all counts, I deserve it. While unforgettable, the year has also been exhausting.

■ ■ ■

A friend asked me what I've learned from my full-immersion truth vow. Where do I begin? For starters, I'm more honest in prayer. This thing about trying to impress God was laughable. I've also learned how far short I land trying to rig things on my own. I speak the truth more speedily now, less concerned with what people say about me when I'm out of earshot. I've learned to be kinder to others, having never walked around in their slippers. And I've learned to appreciate the words of the great American theologian Tim McGraw: "Live like you were dying."[1]

You see, one of the grandest illusions I've allowed myself is that of my own invincibility. With my parents' passing comes thanksgiving for each moment and a renewed awareness that we all leave a legacy. Proverbs 10:7 says, "The memory of the just is blessed." I like that. I think we leave behind a blessed memory when we live with eternity in the viewfinder.

And finally, after completing a year of truth-telling, I'm much more aware of my flaws and weaknesses. Tabulating one's own sins causes the faults of others to fade in significance, so I'm learning the joy of scratching a little deeper beneath the surface of God's grace. What I've found is that there is a God who smiles, a God who still loves me. With his help, I've decided to extend the deadline on this truth vow another fifty years.

Someone asked me the other day if I'll ever tell a lie again. I said, "Probably... Wait, yes, I'm sure I will." I know too much about my inner workings to deceive myself into thinking that I have this problem licked. But I don't think I can lie again without a sense of sorrow and a longing for the joy and peace of an honest life.

■ ■ ■

I have mentioned a number of people in this book, from lifelong friends to beloved family members to people I know only through e-mail correspondence. And as you might expect, life for these folks goes on.

After meeting a nice Christian girl who will not abide smoking, Paul hasn't taken a puff for three months. I hope they hurry up and get married for eighty years.

I've managed to make a few more Mormon friends, including my daughter's schoolmate, who is often in our home. I still haven't heard from the Mormon Church headquarters, though that may change when this book is published.

My former friend and I have started to talk again. I'm ecstatic. Some things come back when you set them free.

I am privileged to continue corresponding with my e-mail friend, the pet care atheist (whose name I have protected). Not a single day has passed without me praying that God will pursue him and that Christians will love him.

About every third Wednesday, I spend half an hour playing Pac-Man. Twice I have reached 150,000 points, switched off the computer, and said, "Ha! I won!" And here is my secret for attaining such proficiency: I listen to Internet sermons as I play. Really. You just push the M key, which silences the game, and you can hear John Piper or Tim Keller or some guy debating atheists. Your game improves and you learn something.

Kevin and his wife said a gut-wrenching good-bye to their darling daughter Alyssa, and our friend Kathy passed through heaven's gates this past November. I'm told that the dessert buffet there never ends.

And after ninety-five dates, Jordan, my daughter's man-friend, knelt and proposed. A summer wedding is on the way.

■ ■ ■

Ramona interrupts my thoughts. "I loved your mama," she says. "You have her eyes, you know. Kind eyes. It was the first thing I liked about you."

"Not my well-toned body? My razor-sharp wit?"

She shakes her head and smiles. Nearby the frog chorale is rehearsing, causing Mojo's ears to stand on end.

"Maybe things will go back to normal now," I say.

"I hope not. I like the more honest you. And I hope the surprises keep coming."

"Oh, they will. I'm sure."

"It's been a good year." Ramona is stirring the iced tea. "Mom is safe Home."

"It can be done."

"What can be done?"

"Living and dying. With integrity. With hope. I'd like to do that."

"You already are," Ramona says.

"I can't believe you married me," I say. I'm being honest, of course.

The sun has almost surrendered to the horizon. A few stubborn rays shine through rocky outcrops, shimmering over the patchwork wheat fields, casting long shadows into the misty hollows and tucking the world in. Like the grace that has covered me all along the way.

# Talking About Telling the Truth

## *How to Get More Out of* To Be Perfectly Honest

Phil Callaway's yearlong attempt to tell the truth is entertaining, informative, inspiring, and at times convicting. There is much to be learned from reading the stories of a person who did his best to be truthful—no matter the situation—for twelve straight months. And that's how these discussion questions can help.

This multisession study will guide you in exploring God's work in your own life. The discussion guide is designed to be used in a variety of ways. You can refer to it informally, when talking over coffee with a friend or your spouse. It's also handy for more intentional settings, such as a book-group discussion or small-group study. The topics and questions are applicable to anyone who is interested in living with more integrity, cutting fewer corners, and putting truthfulness first.

Each discussion focuses on one chapter in the book, but feel free to skip around and discuss the topics and questions that are most relevant to your life, your challenges and questions, and your interests. The questions are designed to encourage open discussion without putting anyone on the spot. The goal is to share with others as you explore God's work in your life.

## Discussion 1: Starting Blocks

1. If you are about to accept the challenge of lieless living, what are the potential problems that come to mind? Be honest.

2. Here's an easy way to rate your HQ (Honesty Quotient):
   a. Here's how to tell I'm lying: my lips are moving.
   b. I do not lie, I merely employ Therapeutic Alterations of Reality.
   c. Usually people trust me when my lips are moving.
   d. With God's help, I'm learning to live and speak the truth.

3. On Day 2, Phil divulged that mechanical activities such as mowing the lawn bring out the worst in him. Have you experienced a similar phenomenon? If so, what helps take your mind off criticizing others? (See Philippians 2:3-4.)

4. The author wrote: "Living truthfully delivers clear benefits, like not having to keep my lies straight" (Day 3). Can you relate? Talk about a time when you were caught in a lie.

5. Read James 5:16. Have you ever made something right that you had avoided for years? What happened?

6. On Day 15, Phil revealed, "I realized I wasn't praying to God at all. I was praying to the people, hoping to impress them." How about you? When you are asked to pray in public, to whom do you pray? (See Matthew 6:5-6 for additional guidance.)

7. It's tempting to try to hide our flaws. What is an area of your life that you would rather people not ask about? Why?

8. Reread Day 23. Can you identify with this confession? What distracts you from time spent deepening your life and your walk with God? How are you prepared to deal with it?

9. Consider trying an experiment this week: tell a friend that he or she can ask you about *anything* and promise that you will be honest with your answer. See how it goes.

10. Did you resonate with the "Honest Confession #1" at the end of the first chapter? Why did you come to faith in Christ? If you haven't, what has kept you from it?

## Discussion 2: The Lost Art of Confrontation

1. On the television show *Intervention*, friends and family members confront a person who is addicted to drugs or alcohol (see Day 24). Have you ever confronted someone who was in the wrong? How did it go? What did you learn from the experience?

2. Rate yourself in the CQ (Confronting Quotient) category:
   a. I avoid it any cost. I will not even scold my cat when he climbs the curtains.
   b. I find it easy to admonish little children—if their parents aren't around.
   c. There is nothing I enjoy more than letting others know about their sins.
   d. I dislike it, but will confront a person if necessary.

3. "If thy brother trespass against thee, rebuke him" (Luke 17:3). What should this look like? What should our motives be in rebuking a person? For more insight, read Matthew 18:15–22.

4. Do you find it easier to be honest with people who are close to you or people you don't know well? Why?

5. On Day 43, the author confessed that during a worship service, he had trouble joining in on some of the songs. Have you ever struggled with this? If so, what were the reasons?

6. In chapter 2 we begin to find out about Phil Callaway's struggle with money. What are some things that both God and money promise us (e.g., peace, security, joy)? Has money ever kept its promises to you in any of these areas? Talk about it.

7. The author prepared for a class reunion in chapter 2. Can you identify with his quest to look good at the event? What is one thing you'd like to be involved in during the next ten years that might be fun to tell at a reunion?

8. How much time do you spend wondering what others think of you? In looking back on five decades in ministry, popular author Charles Swindoll told Phil, "I would have cared less about what people thought or said. And I would have cared more about what Scripture said." How do you feel about Swindoll's comment?

9. Phil wrote: "Being right is nice—but it's all a little pointless without good relationships" (see Honest Confession #2). Do you agree? Reflect on this as it relates to the biblical injunction to "speak the truth in love" (see Ephesians 4:15, NLT).

## Discussion 3: How to Tell the Truth and Still Have a Place to Sleep

1. Forty-two percent of Americans have Googled their own names. Have you? Why or why not?

2. If a waitress gave you fifty-five dollars too much in change, which of the following would you do?

    a. Thank God for the blessing and leave the restaurant fast.

    b. Engage in rationalizations about bad service and overpricing, and give her back a twenty.

    c. Return the full amount, but only because it would come out of her salary.

    d. Live the truth and shame the devil.

3. On Days 57 and 78, the author mentioned music in church. Think about a song that has meant a lot to you. What made it meaningful? How are you cultivating a life of private worship during the week?

4. Consider the ramifications of being completely honest in marriage. Are there times when it's a good idea to keep quiet? If so, give an example.

5. According to the American Academy of Matrimonial Lawyers, more than 80 percent of its members have used evidence gathered from Facebook, Twitter, or YouTube in court. How do you deal with temptations such as the one Phil is experiencing in Days 61–62 and Days 64–68?

6. How helpful is it to make a list of the things you would forfeit if you were to have an affair? (See the one Phil put together on Day 67.)

7. Do you have a friend like Chris who helps keep you accountable (see Day 68)? If so, have you thanked him or her? If not, what will it take to find this type of friend?

8. On Day 70, Phil is mowing the lawn when he pictures a former friend who has been spreading lies about him. He admitted: "Today I see his face on the dandelions and take great delight in lopping them off." Did someone come to your mind when you read that confession? Reread the journal entry for Day 72. What would your prayer be?

9. How can the acrostic for THINK (see Day 83) help you know when and how to speak the truth? What would you add or subtract from the list?

10. Reflect on Honest Confession #3 at the end of the third chapter, particularly the third paragraph. Where do you go first when you sin? How does Christ's love "compel us" to walk on with him (see 2 Corinthians 5:14–15, NIV)? How do you respond when a Christian leader admits to walking with a limp?

## Discussion 4: With Friends Like These

1. On Day 89, Phil finds himself wrestling again with anger toward his "former" friend. Can you think of ways that God uses such a situation to help you catch a glimpse of how wicked your own heart is?

2. Is forgiving someone a one-time act or something that needs to be revisited? Rank your FQ (Forgiveness Quotient):

    a. I will forgive my spouse just as soon as the sun rises in the west.

    b. I like to hang on to things for a few days.

    c. It doesn't matter. I'm so old I can't remember who wronged me.

    d. My being forgiven for so much makes it easier for me to forgive others.

3. Check out Day 93. Do you really believe God is big enough to handle your questions—even your anger? What do you think of the chaplain's words: "The opposite of love is indifference"? Is there a word that accurately describes your current relationship with God (e.g., indifferent, loving, frustrated, afraid, angry, distant, close)?

4. On Day 99, Phil speaks at a church where he is confronted by the greeter. What would you say to this guy (the greeter, not Phil)? How many people do you know who have left the church for good because of the way they were treated? What comes to mind when you think of church? Why?

5. Phil asks his son (Day 102) what kind of person he pictures when he thinks of Christians. Read Colossians 3:9–17, writing down the characteristics that *should* describe believers.

6. On Day 108, Phil spoke to a group of nurses. They received him warmly, in sharp contrast to the greeter at church. Is there someone in your life that you have trouble accepting? Why? What can you do to change the situation?

7. What percentage of your time is spent with nonbelievers? What would you say are the things they like about you? What might they dislike?

8. A major biblical prophet said the Messiah would be "numbered with the transgressors" (Isaiah 53:12). In Luke 7:34, Jesus was accused of being "a friend of…sinners." (This was not a compliment!) What steps can you take to be accused of the same?

9. Reread the entry for Day 107 and think about the question that is asked. How would you respond?

10. Revisit Phil's Honest Confession #4 at the end of the chapter. Is there anything you would add or subtract? If so, what?

## Discussion 5: A Wretch Like Me

1. How would you answer the questions Phil asks about Jesus on Day 116? How truthful do you think Jesus was with the pagans? Discuss these questions: Did they laugh at Jesus' jokes? Did he laugh at theirs? Was he the designated driver?

2. Rate yourself in the HOWS category (Hanging Out With Sinners). If you were golfing or interacting with a guy like Larry (see Day 116), how would you react?

    a. Make sure that, above all else, Larry is informed that he is a sinner.

    b. Beat him decisively, both front nine and back nine.

    c. Make sure he looks forward to the next time.

    d. Make sure he knows that you are amazed by grace and will always welcome opportunities to show it to him.

3. On Day 126, Phil introduces us to Paul the smoker. Do you agree that other habits (gossip, slander, greed, disobedience) are more damaging than smoking? Why, or why not?

4. How would you answer the skeptic's question, Why do you go to church? (Day 127.) Or, maybe, why do you not go to church?

5. Is there a "Kevin" (Day 127) in your life—one who has experienced bitter disappointment yet still raises his hands in praise? Read 2 Corinthians 4:17–18. How can looking forward make a difference in the difficulties we face in life? What other steps do you think people such as Kevin have taken?

6. What would you have done with the elderly gentleman (Day 134)? Phil wrote: "In the history of lies, this may be among the most guileless...[and] most productive." Do you agree? Why, or why not?

7. Was there one part of the brief interaction with Chuck Colson that jumped out at you? Anything you agreed or disagreed with? Why?

8. What did you think of Honest Confession #5? Why is it that witnessing makes both believers and nonbelievers nervous?

9. The author wrote: "I am not accepted because I'm so wonderful, but because he is" (Honest Confession #5). Read Ephesians 1:3–7. How should this truth help us deal with others?

## Discussion 6: Looking for a Sign

1. Do you identify with the author when he divulges that "I don't have an anger problem unless bad things happen to me" (Day 152)? Rank yourself in the PQ (Payback Quotient) category. If someone smacks into your car in the parking lot, which of the following, if any, would you do?

    a. Spend every waking moment plotting a way to find him, so you can make his vehicle look like a block of swiss cheese.

    b. Post uncomplimentary photos of her on Facebook and write hateful letters about her to the local newspaper editor.

    c. Stew quietly, never mention it, and take it out on those closest to you.

    d. Give thanks for auto insurance. And be glad you weren't sitting in the car when it happened.

    Now, read 2 Thessalonians 3:15 and reflect on where you stand regarding the Payback Quotient.

2. Read the amazing story in Acts 9:1–9 of how Saul was transformed from a murderer to a man of integrity through the power of Christ. Then ask yourself, "Do I have any unworthy thoughts or behaviors that I think are so deeply ingrained that they can't be changed?" What are they?

3. The author stated that his words to Paul the smoker (see Day 151) were of no help. In contrast, what have others done to help you change damaging habits or harmful ideas?

4. On Day 155, Phil sensed that someone may be gossiping about him. Any ideas on what to do?

5. Take Phil's Internet-addiction test (Day 162). How did you score? What steps are you taking to make yourself accountable? When you do, what happens? Does it make you feel strong, weak, confident? How can choosing to be accountable protect you from bad decisions and even strengthen the person you are accountable to?

6. Reread Days 158 and 163. What are your thoughts on the TV preacher's words? Have you ever prayed the words, "God, make me rich"? Why, or why not?

7. If you have ever been presented with a wonderful "ground floor" financial opportunity, did you go for it? Why, or why not?

8. Are you the real deal (see Day 171), or are you fake? If fake, are you fake fake or genuine fake? Rate yourself and explain the rating.

9. Read Honest Confession #6. Phil said, "I have liked money all my life." What would your honest confession be if you were asked about money?

## Discussion 7: Angels for Christmas

1. After Paul stops smoking (Day 179), Phil wrote, "Thank you, God! If you can change Paul, there's hope for me!" Is there someone in your life that you would say this about? Why?

2. It's time to rate your Giving Rationale (GR):
    a. Hey, I earned this money. It's mine.
    b. I lend it out with great interest.
    c. I give 10 percent, but not a penny more.
    d. Everything I have is God's. When I see a need, I love to meet it if I can.

3. Do you think the author's joke on the church visitor's card (Day 183) was funny? Or is there no place for such a thing in church?

4. Have you ever sent or received an over-the-top Christmas letter like the one Phil describes on Day 191? Why do people so often engage in the sin of comparison?

5. Is there a family like the Fergusons in your life? Have you considered ways you can love them?

6. Read Hebrews 13:2, 5, 16. Is there a lonely person in your life like the one the author met on Day 196? What is your response to this individual? What should it be?

7. Reread the entry for Day 198. How did your thinking process change about the Fergusons, and why?

8. Have you ever attended church primarily because you were concerned about what people might assume if they noticed you were absent (Day 204)?

9. Was the author right in showing Paul grace on Day 205? How would you handle this situation?

10. Read Romans 7:14–8:1. Do you find it difficult to "live without hypocrisy, turn the other cheek, walk the extra mile," etc., as in Honest Confession #7? Name three things that happen when you walk according to the Spirit.

## Discussion 8: Chasing Money, Chasing Grace

1. Are you big on New Year's resolutions? If you make them, how do you do in following through?

2. Rank yourself in the PIC category (Purity In Church):

   a. I seldom notice anything but what is happening on stage and in the heavenlies.

   b. I am sometimes distracted by bulletin bloopers, such as "Tonight at 6: Sin & Share."

      c. Like Phil, I admit that I have thought of such things as my financial investments during a perfectly good sermon (see Day 211).

3. Helen Roseveare, a missionary doctor whose life has impacted millions, once advised the author: "Above all else, take daily quiet time apart with God. Let nothing squeeze this out of your timetable." Why is this important? How are you doing in this area?

4. Was there a time in your life when you were caught lying or stealing? How did it turn out? Were you forgiven by the offended party?

5. In Matthew 23, Jesus reserves his most condemning language for religious leaders. Why do you think the sin of hypocrisy was so despicable to Jesus?

6. How would you respond if a former friend tried to get you fired from your job?

7. Have you ever considered the "burdens" of money (see Day 234)? Are you still willing to be smitten with it? Why or why not? Read and reflect on Proverbs 30:7–9.

8. What is your response when a friend you are helping and praying for experiences a disappointing setback (see Day 238)?

9. In Honest Confession #8 (and on Days 214 and 222), the author admitted his struggle with envy. Do you find it easier to weep with others or to rejoice with them? What are some steps you can take to genuinely rejoice with those who rejoice, to improve your "party skills"?

## Discussion 9: A Thawing, Outside and In

1. Reread the entry for Day 239 and rank yourself in the RD (Real Deal) category:

a. I'm so plastic, friends call me Bubble Wrap.

b. I'm learning to be more honest with myself, others, and God.

c. I've gone overboard—I can't stop talking about my faults.

d. I'm a little like the old preacher, living a thankful life and constantly amazed by God's grace.

2. In what ways do you think a life of transparent honesty and integrity can help thaw us out? (See, as one example, the entry for Day 248.) In our relationship with God? With others? What obstacles do you anticipate as you live this way?

3. On Day 247, the author found out that the Internet scheme he invested in "may not be entirely aboveboard." Had you already guessed this? Why? What are practical steps we can take to keep from being taken in?

4. Have you ever tried to make a financial deal with God, promising that you'd be extra generous if he would only bless you with a lot more money? How did that work out?

5. Are you an "I told you so" kind of person (Day 249)? Or have you managed to purge those words from your vocabulary?

6. Jesus taught us to pray for our enemies (see Matthew 5:44). How does praying for them change your heart (Day 241), and why does that happen?

7. During a comedy routine in Las Vegas, Jerry Seinfeld said, "They say that what happens in Vegas stays in Vegas. It's a lie. The only thing that stays in Vegas is your money." Reflect on the truth in this statement. How does it relate to the wisdom of Proverbs 5:7–14?

8. Have you ever been in a situation like Phil was on Day 258? What kinds of things do you tend to whine about and

why? How does focusing on 1) the needs of others and 2) what you have to be thankful for, change a tendency to whine?

9. Some might think Phil's prayer (Day 264) is too blunt. Do you agree? Are you confident that God is big enough to handle our honesty—and even our hostility? Why, or why not? What do you think of the author's statement "I love you, but I have trouble understanding you"?

10. The author admits that "sometimes Christians drive me nuts" (Honest Confession #9). Can you identify with his confession? Do you agree with his solution? What would you add?

## Discussion 10: My Judgment Day

1. When was the last time you judged someone (Day 267), only to find out you were wrong about the person? Why do we find it so easy to overlook our own faults and judge others?

2. If a person you once considered a friend was spreading lies about you, would you respond with any of these actions?

   a. Put sugar in his or her gas tank.

   b. Spread a few lies about the liar.

   c. Stew, whine, and become bitter about it.

   d. Confront him or her, then get on with praying for and forgiving the person.

3. Do you have a "Lauren" in your life—one who is facing daunting challenges with great courage? What has this person taught you?

4. The author confides some of his struggles in helping his mother through dementia[1] (see Day 277). What are some of your honest questions for God when it comes to suffering?

5.  On Day 281, Phil relates how someone was impacted by something he said. When God uses you, are you surprised, grateful, proud, inspired, encouraged? Discuss.

6.  Have you ever fallen for the tricks of someone like the e-mail correspondent who identified herself as "Ruth Madoff"? Why do so many succumb to such schemes? Why do the ones who write such e-mails usually employ religious terminology and God's name?

7.  Dietrich Bonhoeffer wrote: "Anybody who has once been horrified by the dreadfulness of his own sin that nailed Jesus to the Cross will no longer be horrified by even the rankest sins of a brother."[2] Reflect on his words in relation to Matthew 7:1–5.

8.  On Days 292 and 293, the author experiences bitter disappointment. What does it take for our disappointments to make us bitter? How can they make us better?

## Discussion 11: Up and Away

1.  How should a deeper realization of God's amazing grace shape us into the image of his Son?

2.  How would you respond to the question posed on Day 305: "What religion are you?" Do you agree with Phil's response? Why, or why not?

3.  In 2 Corinthians 9:8 we read: "And God is able to make all grace abound to you, so that having all sufficiency in all things at all times, you may abound in every good work" (ESV). How have you seen this at work in your life?

4.  How would you respond to criticism of the sort that Phil received on Day 309?

5.  Do you have a pet? If so, does the Rapture as outlined in 1 Thessalonians 4:15–17 worry you?

6. Phil admits on Day 314 that he has been "dumping on God a little more, and I think he likes it." Do you think a person's prayers change as he or she lives a more authentic life? How?

7. Do you know an atheist or agnostic? If so, how would you characterize your relationship?

8. Do you have a "Kathy" (Day 314) in your life? What could you do for her or him this week?

9. Phil has been writing for twenty years, but prior to this book, he had never mentioned in print that he has a brother who lives on the streets (see Day 317). Why do we often pretend things are fine when they aren't? What are the benefits of being open about such challenges and hurts?

10. Reread Honest Confession #11 and reflect on what Phil means by this: "The result is that I neither swagger nor snivel."

## Discussion 12: Insomnia, Mormons, and More Angels

1. What do you find are the main impediments to keeping your word? Pride? Inconvenience? Embarrassment? Insecurity? Fear? What can you do to reprogram your integrity level?

2. How would you define integrity?
    a. not getting caught doing something wrong
    b. being able to accurately evaluate the honesty of others
    c. adhering to God's principles, keeping my promises, and being in private what I appear to be in public

3. Sir William Temple said, "When I pray, coincidences happen, and when I don't, they don't." How does this relate to your life and to Phil's story on Day 338?

4. Proverbs 19:17 says, "Mercy to the needy is a loan to GOD, and GOD pays back those loans in full" (MSG). What is your response to people like Eddie (Day 341)? What are the difficulties you face in helping such people?

5. The author could have saved a whopping $1,500 per year (Day 345) just by telling a simple lie. What would you have done in a similar situation, and why? (Read and discuss Proverbs 19:1–5, 22; and in The Message, Proverbs 20:10.)

6. Phil reignites his conversation with the atheist on Day 352. How does being honest with those who don't share our faith give us more credibility when we bear witness?

7. On Day 353, Phil thanked his mom for such great memories and admits, "I'd like to have said these things...years ago." What should you say to a loved one this week that you wish you'd said often in the past?

8. Read and reflect on Proverbs 20:7, which teaches that being loyal to God and living an honest life makes it much easier on your children. How can living an authentic life lighten your offspring's burdens and be the best legacy you can leave them?

9. How do you respond when you lose money as the author did in his investment?

10. Of the seven things God hates (listed in Proverbs 6:16–19), how many involve a violation of integrity?

## Discussion 13: Safe at Home

1. Has the death of a loved one caused you to "lose" someone close to you? If so, how has this changed the way you live today?

2. On Day 360, the author removes his mother's belongings in four grocery bags. What are the benefits of leaving few

earthly possessions behind? What do you hope to leave behind?

3. The Bible tells us that "all have sinned, and come short of the glory of God" (Romans 3:23). If you have been less than a person of integrity, how can you reboot your integrity computer? Write down a prayerful plan of action that reflects the kind of person you choose to be from today onward.

4. Why is the road to integrity such a tough one? What disciplines should you engage in to become the person you know you should be six months from now? Write down your goals and show them to a friend.

5. Proverbs 10:7 says, "A good and honest life is a blessed memorial" (MSG). Why is an honest life worth remembering? How has this book helped you determine to live such a life? How would you like to be remembered?

# NOTES

## Chapter 1

1. Philippians 4:8 says, "Finally, brothers and sisters, whatever is true, whatever is noble, whatever is right, whatever is pure, whatever is lovely, whatever is admirable—if anything is excellent or praiseworthy—think about such things."

2. This collection of brief allusions to ABBA song lyrics includes:

   "Mamma Mia," by Benny Andersson, Björn Ulvaeus, and Stig Anderson, copyright © 1975, EMI Grove Park Music;

   "Does Your Mother Know," by Benny Andersson and Björn Ulvaeus, copyright © 1979, EMI Grove Park Music;

   "Thank You for the Music," by Benny Andersson and Björn Ulvaeus, copyright © 1977, EMI Waterford Music;

   "I Do, I Do, I Do, I Do, I Do," by Benny Andersson, Björn Ulvaeus, Stig Anderson, copyright © 1975, EMI Grove Park Music;

   "Knowing Me, Knowing You," by Benny Andersson, Björn Ulvaeus, Stig Anderson, copyright © 1976, EMI Grove Park Music;

   "As Good as New," by Benny Andersson and Björn Ulvaeus, copyright © 1979, EMI Grove Park Music.

   The singing group gave an honest response when asked if $1 billion would be enough to get them to reunite. "That's only $250 million each." To this day I can recite the bulk of dozens of ABBA tunes but cannot remember my license plate number, most Scripture references, or my brother Tim's birthday.

3. If you haven't read the parable of the Pharisee and the Tax Collector (Luke 18:9–14) for a while, it's a great reminder of the contrast between self-righteousness and humility in prayer. My Anglican friend Douglas smiles when I confess my difficulty praying in public. He usually crafts his prayers beforehand. They are concise, relevant, and filled with Scripture. This method also removes a number of temptations, including excessive length, overuse of words like "Father," and "I just really really wanna...," and the lure to use prayer as an opportunity to advertise your business publicly as I once heard a man do.

4. Caitlin Flanagan, "Is There Hope for the American Marriage?" *Time*, July 2, 2009.

## Chapter 2

1. Luke 17:3.

2. Kelly Carpenter, "Draw Me Close to You," copyright © 1994, Mercy/Vineyard.

3. Matt Redman, "How Lovely Is Your Dwelling Place (Better Is One Day)," Thankyou Music, 1995.

4. Darlene Zschech, "Shout to the Lord," copyright © 1993, Hillsong.

5. Chris Tomlin and Jesse Reeves, "Glorious," © Copyright 2006 worshiptogether.com Songs/sixsteps Music (admin. by EMI CMG Publishing).

6. Robert Robinson, "Come, Thou Fount of Every Blessing," 1758.

## Chapter 3

1. The only changes I made to this letter were to change the location of the tour bus and clean up some punctuation.

2.  To my surprise, when friends learned that I was writing this book, one mentioned Abraham's lie (see Genesis 12:10–20), and at least three friends reminded me of the story of Rahab (see Joshua 2). One intimated that the lesson to be learned was that lying is okay as long as no one is hurt. Theologians have long debated whether the story of Rahab means that God condones lying, which a few hundred Scripture verses condemn, as does one of the Ten Commandments. I have never seen it this way. Though it doesn't surprise me that a prostitute living in a pagan environment would lie to government authorities, God never applauded her for the lie, nor was she saved because of it. We'll have to wait for heaven to hear the rest of Rahab's story, but we do know from Hebrews 11 that she was saved because of her faith (see also Joshua 2:8–13). My mother mentioned this to me several times after I told whopping fibs, and she was right.

3.  Now in his seventies, George Verwer is still a fireball speaker. He's the founder of the international discipleship and training organization Operation Mobilization and a friend who is helping me with honesty. In his book *Drops from a Leaking Tap,* this giant of the faith tells how he can be honest with his wife: "I report my occasional struggle to her and she does not condemn me. I remember telling her, now as an older man, that a quick glimpse at pornography had caused quite a stir in me physically. 'Well,' she said, 'at least it proves you've got something left.'" (George Verwer, *Drops from a Leaking Tap* [Colorado Springs: Authentic Books, 2008], 78.)

4.  Verwer, *Leaking Tap,* 78.

## Chapter 4

1.  I owe musician and author Bryan Duncan a cup of stiff coffee for the first two sentences of this letter. I have loved Bryan's

honest music through the years, and when we connected during the writing of this book, he told me that I am not alone in my frustrations with people. Yes, we both know we are to be known by our love, but sometimes we aren't.

2. Quotes taken from *The Invention of Lying*, directed by Ricky Gervais and Matthew Robinson (Burbank, CA: Warner Bros. Pictures, 2009).

3. I have considered writing a book about my crazy road adventures, but likely won't. A few days after this event, the pastor called to apologize again. He had had a talk with the gentleman, only to discover that the greeter had masterminded two church splits already that year. I can still see him seated front row center, throwing darts with his eyes as I spoke on the joy that Christ can give. He wasn't buying a word of it and looked so sour that he looked like he could suck rivets off a skateboard. How sad. D. L. Moody once said, "The Lord gives His people perpetual joy when they walk in obedience to Him."

4  For more on the Grants and their ministry, visit www.project rescue.com.

## Chapter 5

1. To read more of Phil Callaway's interview with Chuck Colson, see "Innerview: Why Faith Matters," *Servant*, no. 84 (2010): 10–11, http://www.prairie.edu/servant/Servant%2084.pdf. Note: The questions that Phil asks in the parts of the interview documented in this book are more conversational and do not conform exactly to the text in *Servant* magazine.

## Chapter 6

1. C. S. Lewis, *The Weight of Glory* (San Francisco: HarperOne, 2001), 26.

2. Proverbs 30:7–9, NLT.

## Chapter 7

1. Psalm 137:9.
2. Numbers 6:24–26.
3. For more on this idea, see Romans 7:14–25.

## Chapter 8

1. Steven Curtis Chapman, "Yours," copyright © 2007, Peach Hill Songs.
2. Psalm 35:1–2, 4, 6, 8, 9–10.
3. Proverbs 23:4, MSG and Proverbs 28:20, NKJV.
4. Matthew 5:16, NKJV.
5. See Philippians 4:8.
6. 1 Thessalonians 5:17.
7. I have told this story to a few friends, one of whom said, "Sure, you're making that up." I was able to present a witness who observed the whole thing from the backseat. There are benefits to always traveling with a friend or family member, as I have done for many years.

## Chapter 10

1. Stuart Townend, "How Deep the Father's Love for Us," copyright © 1995, Thankyou Music.
2. The Steve Miller Band, "The Joker," copyright 1973, Cotillion Music.
3. Of course, while the sender claims to be married to former financier Bernie Madoff, one has to seriously question that assertion. One also must assume that her actual name is not Ruth Madoff. However, this is how we will identify her since that is the name she uses in her e-mail correspondence.
4. Dietrich Bonhoeffer, *Life Together: A Discussion of Christian Fellowship* (San Francisco: HarperCollins, 1954), 118.

## Chapter 11

1. Luke 19:9, NIV.
2. 1 Peter 1:4, NIV.
3. Ernest Hemingway, *The Complete Short Stories of Ernest Hemingway* (New York: Simon & Schuster, 1997), 29.
4. Psalm 113:5–8, NLT.
5. Isaac Watts, "O God, Our Help in Ages Past," 1719, music by William Croft, 1708, public domain. This great old hymn was sung at the funeral of former British prime minister Winston Churchill in St. Paul's Cathedral, London, in 1965. Reading about Isaac Watts reminds me of certain elements of my childhood and my attempt to work humor into my writing. Watts took no small degree of heat for his hymns, as many of them did not directly quote Scripture.
6. Timothy Keller, *The Reason for God* (New York: Riverhead, 2008), 187.

## Chapter 12

1. Several excellent books are helping me on this journey. I highly recommend *The Reason for God* by Timothy Keller (New York: Riverhead, 2008) and *Finding an Unseen God* by Alicia Britt Chole (Bloomington, MN: Bethany, 2009).
2. Acts 8:39, NIV.

## Chapter 13

1. Matt Redman and Beth Redman, "Blessed Be Your Name," copyright 2002, Thankyou Music.
2. Kevin graciously gave me permission to reprint his poem. You can read this family's moving story at http://www.wycliffe.ca/wordalive/pdf/wam_2010_penner.pdf.

## Epilogue

1. Tim McGraw, "Live Like You Were Dying," by Tim Nichols and Craig Wiseman, copyright © 2004, Curb Songs.

## Discussion Questions

1. I tell this story in greater detail in my book *Family Squeeze: Tales of Hope and Hilarity for a Sandwiched Generation* (Colorado Springs: Multnomah, 2008).
2. Dietrich Bonhoeffer, *Life Together: A Discussion of Christian Fellowship* (San Francisco: HarperCollins, 1954), 118.